VOA
Science &
Technology
Report

Junko Murao   Akiko Miyama   Judy Noguchi

VOA で学ぶ最先端技術と PBL 基礎演習

音声ファイルのダウンロード／ストリーミング

CD マーク表示がある箇所は、音声を弊社 HP より無料でダウンロード／ストリーミングすることができます。トップページのバナーをクリックし、書籍検索してください。書籍詳細ページに音声ダウンロードアイコンがございますのでそちらから自習用音声としてご活用ください。

https://www.seibido.co.jp

VOA Science & Technology Report

はじめに

　本書は、国内外において、海外の学生と共同でプロジェクトに取り組んだり、研究をしたりする交流が盛んになっている昨今、その活動を英語で行うために必要な英語のスキルを養成する目的で作成されています。このようないわゆる PBL (Problem-Based Learning) と称される活動の中で、現地の学生と、または国内で海外からの留学生と共に活動を英語で行うことは、英語を修得するのに非常に有効な方法です。また、プロジェクトを進めるにあたって、スケジュールを調整したり、計画を立てたり、問題点を指摘したり、提案をしたりといったやり取りを行うことで、モチベーションを高め、社会人としての基礎力や他人と協働できる能力といった幅広いスキルを同時に養うこともできます。しかし、そのようなやり取りを行う英語の基礎知識がないまま PBL 活動をいきなり行うことは困難です。そのため PBL English をある程度身につけてから、プロジェクトに参加することが必須でしょう。本書は、実際にプロジェクトを行うにあたって必要な英語の知識を構築する目的で作成しました。

　複数のメンバーと共に取り組むプロジェクトでは、問題を発見し、解決し、実践し、検証しながら完成を目指していく一連の作業工程を繰り返すことになります。この問題発見と解決に至るプロセスは、Plan（計画）、Do（実行）、Check（評価）、Action（改善）と言い表され、略して PDCA サイクルと呼ばれます。本書では、世界で発信されている様々な技術について書かれた記事を読み、読解力を養成しながら、この4つの PDCA サイクルの各段階に必要な何らかのプロジェクトを想定した会話表現が学べるよう構成されています。それぞれの段階につき5章が割り当てられ、5章目は各段階のまとめの章となっています。

　章の構成と各アクティビティは以下のようになります。まずは Reading セクションを読むために必要な知識の構築と、その内容読解問題で内容理解の確認をします。

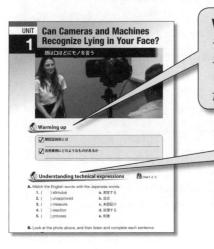

Warming up
テーマについての背景知識を構築するアクティビティです。テーマに関して調べたり、ディスカッションしたりします。

Understanding technical expressions
本文に出てくる専門基礎語彙やフレーズを学びます。
A　記事を読むために必要な主要語彙
B　記事を読むために必要な主要フレーズ。音声を聞いて答えを確認します。

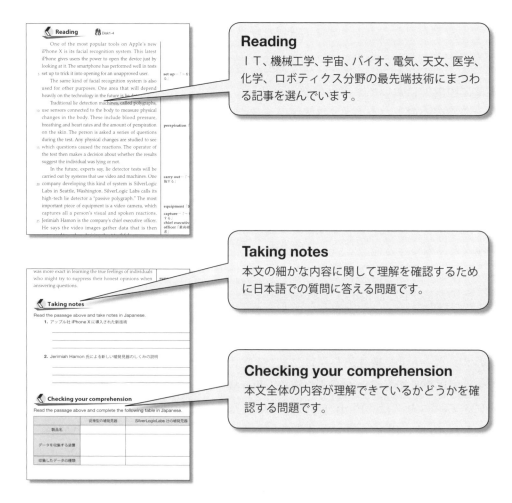

Reading
ＩＴ、機械工学、宇宙、バイオ、電気、天文、医学、化学、ロボティクス分野の最先端技術にまつわる記事を選んでいます。

Taking notes
本文の細かな内容に関して理解を確認するために日本語での質問に答える問題です。

Checking your comprehension
本文全体の内容が理解できているかどうかを確認する問題です。

ここからが実践のパートになります。Reading に取り上げたトピックスに関連するプロジェクトに基づいて、PDCA サイクルの各段階に必要な会話表現を学びます。会話形式になっていますので、プロジェクトの一員になったつもりでロールプレイをしてみます。

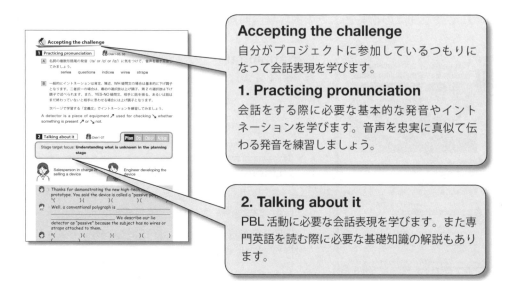

Accepting the challenge
自分がプロジェクトに参加しているつもりになって会話表現を学びます。

1. Practicing pronunciation
会話をする際に必要な基本的な発音やイントネーションを学びます。音声を忠実に真似て伝わる発音を練習しましょう。

2. Talking about it
PBL 活動に必要な会話表現を学びます。また専門英語を読む際に必要な基礎知識の解説もあります。

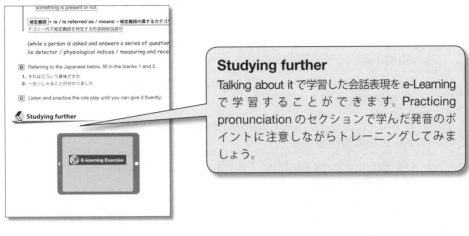

Studying further

Talking about it で学習した会話表現を e-Learning で学習することができます。Practicing pronunciation のセクションで学んだ発音のポイントに注意しながらトレーニングしてみましょう。

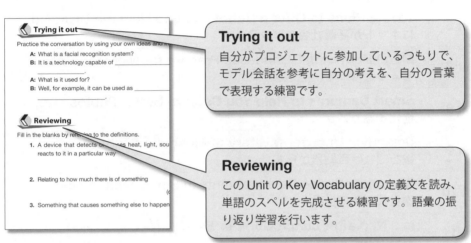

Trying it out

自分がプロジェクトに参加しているつもりで、モデル会話を参考に自分の考えを、自分の言葉で表現する練習です。

Reviewing

この Unit の Key Vocabulary の定義文を読み、単語のスペルを完成させる練習です。語彙の振り返り学習を行います。

本書では、グローバルな視点を養いながら、同時に未来の社会を展望できるようなトピックスを鋭意選択しています。記事はすべて VOA（Voice of America）Science Report からの抜粋でサイエンスとテクノロジーの記事が中心となっていますが、理系および文系の学習者両方に利用が可能となっています。本書を学ぶことによって、国際社会の一員として活躍できる英語コミュニケーション・スキルが磨ける一助となれば幸いです。

本書の作成にあたり、株式会社成美堂の宍戸貢氏には大変お世話になりました。この場をお借りして著者一同感謝の辞を述べたいと思います。

著者一同

CONTENTS

	INPUT
	Reading
Unit 1	**Can Cameras and Machines Recognize Lying in Your Face?** 顔は口ほどにモノを言う
Unit 2	**How Will Machines and AI Change the Future of Work?** AI 時代に生き残る方法
Unit 3	**Doctors Use Virtual Reality to Prepare for Surgeries** VR が変える医療
Unit 4	**US Businesses Making Farming Technologies for Cities** 都市型農業の未来
Unit 5	***Origami* Space Technology Combines Art, Design, Science** 日本の伝統芸が NASA で大活躍
Unit 6	**Toyota Plans to Offer a Robotic Leg to Help the Disabled** ロボットが高齢社会をアシスト
Unit 7	**Metal Recycling Businesses Prepare for More Electric Cars** ちょっと待って、捨てないで
Unit 8	**Smart Cameras to Help You Capture Better Photos** 進化するカメラ
Unit 9	**Scientists Uncover Mystery of Mosquito Flight** 敵を知れば百戦殆からず
Unit 10	**Scientists Praise Developments in Smell Technology** 次世代 VR の世界
Unit 11	**Is a Nap after Lunch Good or Bad?** 昼寝の効能とは？
Unit 12	**Smart Mirrors Show What You Would Look Like Wearing Those Earrings** 進化するスマートフォンアプリ
Unit 13	**Glowing Cancer Cells Easier to Find and Remove** 癌細胞を光らせる
Unit 14	**Meet CIMON, a 'Floating' Space Assistant for Astronauts** 宇宙に AI が行く時代
Unit 15	**Do Bats Hold the Secret to Long Life?** コウモリが教える老化の意味
Unit 16	**New Battery-Free Cellphone Is Powered by Radio Signals** もう電池残量を気にしなくていい？
Unit 17	**Distant Star Refuses to Die** 星は死ぬのか
Unit 18	**Coffee to Help Power London's Buses** コーヒーがロンドンを変える
Unit 19	**British Start-Up Uses Feathers to Make Building Materials** 驚異の天然材料
Unit 20	**As Web Turns 30, Creator Calls for Big Changes to Make It Better** インターネットの未来は？

OUTPUT

Practicing pronunciation	Talking about It (Stage target focus)	
/s/, /z/,/iz/ の発音 イントネーション	Understanding what is unknown in the planning stage	**p.1**
"th"(/θ/ /ð/)の発音 ポーズを入れて発音	Identifying sub-tasks or sub-problems of the project	**p.7**
ライト L、ダーク L の発音 強弱のリズム	Proposing necessary steps in performing the plan	**p.13**
and の発音の変化 ニュアンスで変わる and の発音	Exchanging ideas at the planning stage	**p.19**
/t/ の発音 名詞＋ of のリンキングの発音	Planning a new product using origami-based technology	**p.25**
"-y"、"y-" の発音 文中における "y-" の音の変化	Deciding on the framework of a project	**p.31**
/b/, /v/ の発音 口の形や舌の位置が近い単語が続く場合の発音 (1)	Clarifying detailed information concerning the project	**p.37**
/n/ の発音 弱母音 /ə/ の発音	Allotting responsibility in the project	**p.43**
/s/, /ʃ/ の発音 リダクションの発音	Giving instructions to the members of a project	**p.49**
/ŋ/ の発音 子音と母音のリンキングの発音	Developing a new product using smell technology	**p.55**
母音 /i:/, /u:/ の発音 前置詞句のつながる音	Identifying problems	**p.61**
"t"の flapping and や or を含む文章のイントネーション	Discussing solutions	**p.67**
母音 /e/, /æ/ の発音 冠詞や前置詞のリンキング	Making suggestions for improvement	**p.73**
"y" 以外のつづり字の /j/ の発音 リズミカルに英語を読む	Reporting how the plan is progressing	**p.79**
/r/, とライト L の発音 口の形や舌の位置が近い単語が続く場合の発音 (2)	Checking the process of experimental procedures using specimens	**p.85**
/h/, /hw/ の発音 シャドーイングについて	Checking the operation of the equipment	**p.91**
口の形や舌の位置が同じ有声音と無声音 リピーティングについて	Implementing the revised plan	**p.97**
二重母音 /au/, /ou/ の発音 意味の区切りを意識して文を読む	Testing the revised plan	**p.103**
二重母音 /ei/ の発音 分からない単語は辞書を調べて発音	Checking the results of the plan	**p.109**
/w/ の発音 身に付けてきたスキルを使って発音	Confirming the performance of a new software program	**p.115**

EnglishCentralのご案内

本テキスト各ユニットの「Talking about it」で学習する音声は、オンライン学習システム「EnglishCentral」で学習することができます。EnglishCentralでは動画の視聴や単語のディクテーションのほか、動画のセリフを音読し録音すると、コンピュータが発音を判定します。PCだけでなく、スマートフォンのアプリからも学習できます。リスニング、スピーキング、語彙力向上のため、ぜひ活用してください。

EnglishCentralの利用にはアカウントとアクセスコードの登録が必要です。登録方法については下記ページにアクセスしてください。

（画像はすべてサンプルで、実際の教材とは異なります）

https://www.seibido.co.jp/np/englishcentral/blended.html

本文内でわからなかった単語は1クリックでその場で意味を確認

スロー再生

日英字幕（ON/OFF可）

音声を聴いて空欄の単語をタイピング。ゲーム感覚で楽しく単語を覚える

動画のセリフを音読し録音、コンピュータが発音を判定。

日本人向けに専門開発された音声認識によってスピーキング力を％で判定

ネイティブと自分が録音した発音を聞き比べ練習に生かすことができます

苦手な発音記号を的確に判断し、単語を緑、黄、赤の3色で表示

UNIT 1 Can Cameras and Machines Recognize Lying in Your Face?

顔は口ほどにモノを言う

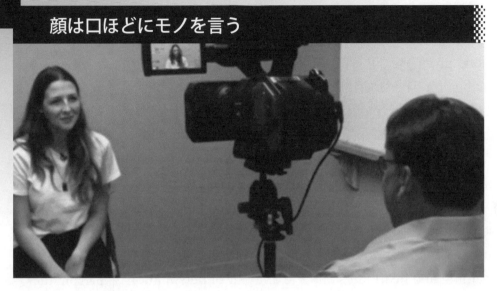

 **Warming up**

☑ 顔認証技術とは
_____

☑ 活用事例にどのようなものがあるか
_____

 Understanding technical expressions 🎧 Disk1-02, 03

A. Match the English words with the Japanese words.

1. (　　　) stimulus   **a.** 測定する
2. (　　　) unapproved   **b.** 反応
3. (　　　) measure   **c.** 未認証の
4. (　　　) reaction   **d.** 処理する
5. (　　　) process   **e.** 刺激

B. Look at the photo above, and then listen and complete each sentence.

1. They (　　　　　　　　) (　　　　　　　　) a test.
   （彼らは、テストを行っている）

2. The facial (　　　　　　　　) technology under (　　　　　　　　) can be used as a high-tech lie (　　　　　　　　) tool.
   （開発中のその顔認証技術は、ハイテク嘘発見器として使うことができる）

 Disk1-04

One of the most popular tools on Apple's new iPhone X is its facial recognition system. This latest iPhone gives users the power to open the device just by looking at it. The smartphone has performed well in tests
5 set up to trick it into opening for an unapproved user.

set up…「～を設定する」

The same kind of facial recognition system is also used for other purposes. One area that will depend heavily on the technology in the future is lie detection.

Traditional lie detection machines, called polygraphs,
10 use sensors connected to the body to measure physical changes in the body. These include blood pressure, breathing and heart rates and the amount of perspiration on the skin. The person is asked a series of questions during the test. Any physical changes are studied to see
15 which questions caused the reactions. The operator of the test then makes a decision about whether the results suggest the individual was lying or not.

perspiration「発汗」

In the future, experts say, lie detector tests will be carried out by systems that use video and machines. One
20 company developing this kind of system is SilverLogic Labs in Seattle, Washington. SilverLogic Labs calls its high-tech lie detector a "passive polygraph." The most important piece of equipment is a video camera, which captures all a person's visual and spoken reactions.
25 Jerimiah Hamon is the company's chief executive officer. He says the video images gather data that is then processed to make a decision about truthfulness.

carry out…「～を実施する」

equipment「装備」
capture…「～を記録する」
chief executive officer「最高経営責任者」

"We're breaking it (footage) down into data and then using quant methods, or quantitative math, and deep
30 learning from the videos to determine how a person's emotional responses are tied to some stimulus. So in this instance, it was questions."

footage「映像」
quant method「定量（分析）法」
determine…「～を決定する」
instance「場合」

This technology is not new. It was first developed to measure the reactions people had while watching movies

2

35 and television shows. Earlier studies showed this method was more exact in learning the true feelings of individuals who might try to suppress their honest opinions when answering questions.

suppress…「～を控える」

 Taking notes

Read the passage and take notes in Japanese.

1. Apple 社 iPhone X に導入された新技術

_____

_____

_____

2. Jerimiah Hamon 氏による新しい嘘発見器のしくみの説明

_____

_____

_____

 Checking your comprehension

Read the passage and complete the following table in Japanese.

	従来型の嘘発見器	SilverLogic Labs 社の嘘発見器
製品名		
データを収集する装置		
収集したデータの種類		

Accepting the challenge

1 Practicing pronunciation  Disk1-05, 06

A 名詞の複数形語尾の発音（/s/ or /z/ or /iz/）に気をつけて、音声を聴き発音してみましょう。

series   questions   indices   wires   straps

B 一般的にイントネーションは肯定、陳述、WH 疑問文の場合は基本的に下げ調子となります。二者択一の場合は、最初の選択肢は上げ調子、第 2 の選択肢は下げ調子で述べられます。また、YES-NO 疑問文、相手に話を振る、あるいは話はまだ終わっていないと相手に思わせる場合には上げ調子となります。

次ページで学習する「定義文」でイントネーションを練習してみましょう。

A detector is a piece of equipment ↗ used for checking ↘ whether something is present ↗ or ↘ not.

2 Talking about it Disk1-07

Plan	Do	Check	Action

Stage target focus: **Understanding what is unknown in the planning stage**

 Salesperson in charge of selling a device

 Engineer developing the device

: Thanks for demonstrating the new high-tech lie detector prototype. You said the device is called a "passive polygraph."
[1.](   ) (   ) (   ) (   )?

: Well, a conventional polygraph is _____
_____. We describe our lie detector as "passive" because the subject has no wires or straps attached to them.

: [2.](   ) (   ) (   ) (   )
(   ).

A　Use the clues below to rearrange the phrases in parentheses, and fill in the underlined part.

Definition（定義文）：プロジェクトの初期段階において未知情報の確認にはしばしば定義文が利用されます。

e.g. **A detector** is <u>a piece of equipment</u> used for checking whether something is present or not.

被定義語 **+ is / is referred to as / means +** <u>被定義語の属するカテゴリー</u> +カテゴリー内で被定義語を特定する形容詞相当語句

(while a person is asked and answers a series of questions/ a lie detector / physiological indices / measuring and recording)

B　Referring to the Japanese below, fill in the blanks 1 and 2.

1. それはどういう意味ですか
2. おっしゃることが分かりました

C　Listen and practice the role play until you can give it fluently.

 Studying further

Trying it out

Practice the conversation by using your own ideas and information.

    A: What is a facial recognition system?

    B: It is a technology capable of _____

    _____.

    A: What is it used for?

    B: Well, for example, it can be used as _____

    _____.

Reviewing

Fill in the blanks by referring to the definitions.

    1. A device that detects or senses heat, light, sound, motion and then reacts to it in a particular way

                        (s _ _ _ _ _)

    2. Relating to how much there is of something

                    (q _ _ _ _ _ _ _ _ _ _)

    3. Something that causes something else to happen

                     (s _ _ _ _ _ _)

How Will Machines and AI Change the Future of Work?

AI 時代に生き残る方法

Warming up

☑ AI とは

☑ AI の導入が進んだら、消える仕事と残る仕事を考えてみよう

Understanding technical expressions

Disk1-08, 09

A. Match the English words with the Japanese words.

1. ( ) estimate	**a.** 証拠
2. ( ) effect	**b.** 可能性
3. ( ) evidence	**c.** 取って代わる
4. ( ) displace	**d.** 予測/推測
5. ( ) potential	**e.** 影響

B. Look at the photo above, and then listen and complete each sentence.

1. An (   ) line laborer works across from a collaborative robot, on the right, at a (   ) facility.
（製造工場で、組み立てラインの作業員が、共同作業ロボット［写真右］の向かいで働いている）

2. The worker is required to react to (   ) (   ).
（作業員は不測の事態に対応する必要がある）

Several recent studies examined how machine automation and artificial intelligence (AI) will change the future of work. Some estimates predict these technologies could displace up to 30 percent of workers worldwide by
5 2030.

One study was published by Pricewaterhouse-Coopers, an international company providing financial and tax services. It predicted about 38 percent of American jobs could be at high risk for automation by the
10 early 2030s. In Germany, up to 35 percent of jobs could be at risk. The company said about 30 percent could be affected in Britain and 21 percent in Japan. "New smart machines have the potential to replace our minds and to move around freely in the world," the study said.

15 The RAND Corporation recently issued its own report on the future effects of automation and AI on jobs and the workplace. Osonde Osoba, a co-author of the report, agrees there will be major job disruptions due to AI and automation, especially for lower-skilled workers.
20 But he told VOA he believes the future problems have been overestimated without historical evidence to back up the predictions.

"It's not so much that the jobs are getting displaced, it's more like tasks are getting displaced and jobs are
25 reconfiguring over time to account for that automation."

The RAND report identifies three job types that will be very difficult to replace with a machine. These include jobs depending on human motor skills, positions requiring creative thinking and actions, and jobs dealing
30 with intense social interaction.

The McKinsey Global Institute, a private think tank, has also studied the issue. Its research suggests that up to one-third of work activities across 46 nations could be displaced by 2030. McKinsey identified several jobs that

financial「金融の」

affect…「～に影響を与える」**smart**「ハイテクの」

issue「発表する」

co-author「共著者」

disruption「解雇」

overestimate…「～を過大評価する」

it's not so much that…「～ということではない」

it's more like…「むしろ～に近い」

reconfigure…「～を再構成する」

account for…「～を担う」

identify…「～を特定する」

motor skills「運動能力」

35　will not be easily replaceable by machines. These include health-care providers, engineers, scientists, accountants, technology experts and managers. It also predicted rising demand for educators, and "creatives," a group of workers including artists, performers and entertainers.

40　The study said automation will also raise productivity and economic growth. It said this growth – along with other economic influences - could help offset the displacement of millions of workers.

provider「業者」
accountant「会計士」

productivity「生産性」

offset「相殺する」

Taking notes

Read the passage and take notes in Japanese.

1. PricewaterhouseCoopers 社の統計による、2030 年代前半までに消える仕事の国別の割合は

_____

_____

_____

2. PricewaterhouseCoopers 社の指摘するハイテク機械の可能性

_____

_____

_____

Checking your comprehension

Read the passage and complete the following table in Japanese.

	RAND Corporation	McKinsey Global Institute
消えない仕事		

Accepting the challenge

1 **Practicing pronunciation**  Disk1-11, 12

A th の音（/θ/ /ð/）は日本語にはない音です。舌を軽く歯の間に挟み込んで発音します。語頭の th は素早く舌を引きながら発音します。音声を聴き発音してみましょう。

the   that   this   with   anything   they

B 長い英文を読むときは、途中に短い休止（ポーズ）を入れながら読みます。長い主語のうしろ、接続詞・前置詞・関係詞の前が区切りの目安となります。以下の文を、スラッシュのところでポーズを入れて読んでみましょう。

Yes, / we also need to know / how they are doing the job now / and how fine the color distinctions need to be.

2 **Talking about it** Disk1-13   **Plan** Do Check Action

Stage target focus: **Identifying sub-tasks or sub-problems of the project**

 Salesperson in charge of selling a device

 Engineer developing the device

: The clients want an _____

_____

_____.

: I see. In order to do this, we [1.](   ) (   )
(   ) have actual examples of the fruits with the color differences.

: OK, I will ask them to provide samples. Anything else?

: Yes, we [2.](   ) (   ) (   )
know how they are doing the job now and how fine the color distinctions need to be.

: Fine. I will contact them about this immediately.

A Use the clues below to rearrange the phrases in parentheses, and fill in the underlined part.

製品・技術を説明する頻出表現（形容詞相当語句の後置修飾）

e.g. AI apps like Google Translate **could replace interpreters in the near future.**

（近い将来グーグル翻訳のような AI アプリが通訳者に取って代わるかもしれない）

製品・技術 ＋ [現在分詞（**Ving**）、過去分詞（**Ved**）、関係詞節、前置詞句]

(between shades of color on the fruit surface / AI device / will be able to distinguish / the fine differences / that)

B Referring to the Japanese below, fill in the blanks 1 and 2.

1. まず～する必要があります

2. ～もする必要があります

C Listen and practice the role play until you can give it fluently.

 Studying further

 **Trying it out**

Practice the conversation by using your own ideas and information.

    A: Hey, did you know that we may be out of job in a couple of years?

    B: _____?

                   （どういうこと？）

    A: Well, if we don't do creative work, we could be replaced by a machine that is more efficient!

    B: Well, I don't know about you, but I _____

    _____.

 **Reviewing**

Fill in the blanks by referring to the definitions.

    1. Force people to move from one place, job, etc. to another

                                                 (d _ _ _ _ _ _ _)

    2. Causing something to be unable to continue in the normal way

                                              (d _ _ _ _ _ _ _ _)

    3. Change the way something is arranged or prepared

                                             (r _ _ _ _ _ _ _ _ _)

UNIT 3

Doctors Use Virtual Reality to Prepare for Surgeries

VR が変える医療

 **Warming up**

☑ **VR 技術とは**

_____

☑ **VR 技術はどんな分野で利用されているか**

_____

 Understanding technical expressions 🖸 Disk1-14, 15

A. Match the English words with the Japanese words.

1. ( ) treat		**a.** 手術する	
2. ( ) operate		**b.** 注射する	
3. ( ) inject		**c.** 修復する	
4. ( ) repair		**d.** 破裂する	
5. ( ) break		**e.** 治療する	

B. Look at the photo above, and then listen and complete each sentence.

1. Felicia Luna is more relaxed after (   ) her aneurysm through (   ) (   ).

   (Felicia Luna さんは、VR を使って動脈瘤を見たあとは以前よりリラックスしている)

2. She talks to her children on the day before her brain (   ).

   (彼女は、脳の手術の 1 日前に子供たちと話をしている)

13

Felicia Luna had a really bad headache. She said the painful pressure felt "like someone was squeezing my head really tight." The pain became so bad that the 41-year-old woman could not lie down and rest her head
5 on a pillow.

Then, she went to the Stanford Medical Center in California. There, she was told doctors needed to operate on an aneurysm in her brain. And they needed to act quickly.

10 Doctor Gary Steinberg said the aneurysm was in danger of breaking. The operation he proposed would be very complex. Luna worried a lot about the treatment. She also wanted to know more about it. So Steinberg decided to use virtual reality technology to improve and
15 explain the surgical operation.

To do this, medical experts needed to take three dimensional (3D) images of Luna's brain. A dye, or colored fluid, was injected into her bloodstream. Doctors then used computerized tomography (CT) technology to
20 make detailed pictures of her brain and blood vessels.

Malie Collins is program coordinator of the Stanford Neurological Simulation and Virtual Reality Center. She creates the VR images Steinberg uses when preparing for surgery.

25 Doctors can see the images using headsets like Oculus Rift or similar devices. Collins trained Stanford's medical workers to use the equipment. Then she joined the team.

Part of Collin's job is to create a "fly through" virtual
30 reality video for patients. It lets them see inside their own bodies. This virtual reality trip lets doctors see what is wrong and how to treat it.

For Felicia Luna, that means she can put on a headset and travel through her own brain. Before the operation,

squeeze…「～を締め付ける」
tight「強く／きつく」

propose…「～を提案する」

surgical「外科の」

dye「染料」
fluid「液体」**inject**…「～を注射する」
bloodstream「血流」

blood vessel「血管」

coordinator「進行係」

fly through…「フライスルー：（臓器の中を）飛び回る」

35 Luna admitted that she was "a nervous wreck." But with the video, she was able to see the path Steinberg would take to repair her blood vessel. "Now I feel like I know exactly what's going to happen."

Collins said the virtual reality tool makes the
40 experience better for the patient, helps the doctor and assists in education. That is what "makes it unique and powerful," she said.

Luna left the hospital two days after the operation to be with her four children and her husband.

nervous wreck「精神的に参っている人」
path「やり方」

Taking notes

Read the passage and take notes in Japanese.

1. 病院へ行く前の Felicia Luna さんの症状

_____

_____

2. VR を使って説明を受ける前と後の Luna さんの反応

_____

_____

Checking your comprehension

Read the passage and complete the sentences.

1. Doctor Gary Steinberg used VR technology
  a. after Luna's brain surgery.　　　**b.** only during Luna's surgery.
  c. before and during Luna's surgery.

2. Malie Collins
  a. trained Luna to use the VR equipment so that she could get pain relief.
  b. thinks of the VR technology as a powerful tool for both doctors and patients.
  c. created a sightseeing travel video to make Luna feel at home.

Accepting the challenge

  Disk1-17, 18

A "l" は後に母音が続く<u>ライトL</u>と呼ばれる場合と、語尾や子音が後に続く<u>ダーク</u> <u>L</u>と呼ばれる場合で発音が異なります。<u>ライトL</u>は舌が歯茎に接した状態で「う ー」とうなってから、舌をはじくことで発音されます。<u>ダークL</u>はうなりが音の 中心になります。音声を聴き発音してみましょう。

p**l**an **l**ike hand**le** we'**ll** **l**eave coi**l**ing

B 英語は、伝えたい部分を強く読んで、特に重要ではない部分は弱く読むという強 弱のリズムを持っています。以下の文の下線部を強調して読んでみましょう。

I'd be <u>happy</u> to <u>handle</u> the <u>preparation</u> of the <u>catheter</u>.

2 **Talking about it**   Disk1-19 | **Plan** | Do | Check | Action |

Stage target focus: **Proposing necessary steps in performing the plan**

  Head surgeon

  Young surgeon supporting the operation

 : The plan _____ the aneurysm. Because we do not have much time,
¹·(   ) (   ) (   ) (   )
(   ) (   ) (   ) (   ).

 : I'd be happy to handle the preparation of the catheter.
²·(   ) (   ) (   ) (   )?

 : OK, so we'll leave that to you. Do you think you can also prepare the coiling?

 : Yes, I can handle that, too.

 : Fine.

Notes: catheter「カテーテル」   coiling「コイル塞栓術」

16

A Rearrange the phrases in the parentheses, and fill in the underlined part.

(to reach / to take / is / this route)

B Referring to the Japanese below, fill in the blanks 1 and 2.

1. 私は作業を分担したい
2. どう思いますか

C Listen and practice the role play until you can give it fluently.

 Studying further

Trying it out

Practice the conversation by using your own ideas and information.

A: What is the advantage of using virtual reality to support surgery?

B: Well, it allows doctors _____

_____ .

A: When do you think the doctors can use the VR technology?

B: They can use it _____ .

Reviewing

Fill in the blanks by referring to the definitions.

1. To put pressure on opposite sides of something

(s _ _ _ _ _)

2. Technology that recreates a place or experience using images, sound and other things

(v _ _ _ _ _ _ r _ _ _ _ _ _)

3. Giving the appearance of an object's height, width and length

(t _ _ _ _ - d _ _ _ _ _ _ _ _ _)

UNIT 4

US Businesses Making Farming Technologies for Cities

都市型農業の未来

Warming up

 垂直農業とは

_____

 垂直農業の利点を考えてみよう

_____

Understanding technical expressions

 Disk1-20, 21

A. Match the English words with the Japanese words.

1. (　　　) fabric　　　　　　　a. 水栽培
2. (　　　) break up　　　　　　b. 柔らかくなる
3. (　　　) hydroponics　　　　c. 分解する
4. (　　　) grouping　　　　　　d. 繊維素材
5. (　　　) soften　　　　　　　e. 配合

B. Look at the photo above, and then listen and complete each sentence.

1. Cam MacKugler, (　　　　　　　　　) of Seedsheet, (　　　　　　　　　)
   (　　　　　　　　) a seedsheet at an event in Brooklyn.
   (Seedsheet 社の創設者、Cam MacKugler 氏が、ブルックリン区で行われた
   あるイベントで、seedsheet に水やりをしている)

2. The (　　　　　　　　　) are for people who live in (　　　　　　　　)
   buildings or other homes with little space for growing plants.
   (その製品は高層ビルや植物を育てるためのスペースが少ない家に住んでいる人向
   けである)

19

How do you get the freshest, locally grown fruits and vegetables in a big city? For an increasing number of Americans, the answer is to grow the fruits and vegetables themselves.

5   Businessman Cam MacKugler can help. He is the founder and chief executive officer of Seedsheet. MacKugler was at the Food Loves Tech event in Brooklyn, New York, earlier this month. He was showing off Seedsheet products, which are for people who live in high-rise buildings or
10 other homes with little space for growing plants.

    Seedsheet products come with fabric sheets and small pods, each filled with a mix of seeds and soil. The fabric is placed on top of dirt in a home planter or in the ground. When watered, the pods soften and eventually
15 break up as the plants start to grow.

    The seed groupings on any given Seedsheet provide vegetables or herbs for salads and other meals. Pricing starts at $15 for the factory-made sheets. But you can spend up to $100 for a larger, made-to-order outdoor
20 covering measuring 1.2 by 2.4 meters.

    Efforts like Seedsheet come as Americans increasingly want to know where their food comes from. Many are looking for socially and environmentally responsible growing methods.

25   American consumers are not giving up on the low cost and ease of packaged and prepared foods. But new products and technologies are playing a part in helping Americans understand where their food comes from.

    "Consumer education is really progressing,"
30 said Nicole Baum of Gotham Greens, a grower of hydroponically grown produce. Baum said consumers were less familiar with the term "hydroponics" — growing plants in water instead of soil — when Gotham Greens first started in 2011.

---

locally「地元で」

come with…「～とセットになっている」
pod「容器」
dirt「土」
eventually「最後には」

any given「任意の」

factory-made「既製の」
made-to-order「注文生産の」

environmentally responsible「環境に責任を持った」

packaged and prepared foods「包装された加工食品」

produce「農産物」

be less familiar with…「～になじみがない」 **term**「言葉」

35   But more and more Americans have since heard about this form of agriculture. The company now provides leafy greens and herbs grown on buildings to supermarkets and top-rated New York restaurants like Gramercy Tavern.

leafy greens「葉物野菜」

Taking notes

Read the passage and take notes in Japanese.

1. Seedsheet とはどのような製品か

_____

_____

_____

2. Gotham Greens 社は何を販売しているか

_____

_____

_____

Checking your comprehension

Read the following sentences about Seedsheet. Decide whether it is T (true) or F (false).

1. (   ) It sells locally grown fruits and vegetables in a big city.

2. (   ) Its founder is developing pods filled with seeds and soil for farmers.

3. (   ) It sells both ready-made and made-to-order products.

4. (   ) Its products are meant to be environmentally friendly.

5. (   ) Its products are provided to a prestigious restaurant in New York City.

Accepting the challenge

1 **Practicing pronunciation**  Disk1-23, 24

A "and" は前後にくる単語により発音が、/ənd/ /ən/ /nd/ /n/ に変化します。音声を聴き発音してみましょう。

bread and butter (/n/)   bread and apples (/nd/)

set it up here and grow them (/ən/)

B and は伝えたいニュアンスによって、同じ文でも発音が変化します。以下の英文の and を強調しないとき (/en/) と、強調するときの and (/ænd/) の区別をして、全文を読んでみましょう。

I'm thinking of setting up a large planter here **and** growing salad greens.

2 **Talking about it**  Disk1-25   **Plan** Do Check Action

Stage target focus: **Exchanging ideas at the planning stage**

 Resident A   Resident B

: I'm thinking of setting up a large planter here and growing salad greens.

: How_____?

: Oh, about 2 x 4 meters.

: That might work, but would it be possible to have two smaller planters? They'd be easier to handle.
1.(   ) (   ) two 1.5 x 2 meter planters?

: 2.(   ) (   ) (   ) (   )!

A Rearrange the phrases in the parentheses, and fill in the underlined part.

(of / are / a / thinking / planter / you / big)

B Referring to the Japanese below, fill in the blanks 1 and 2.

1. 〜はどうですか
2. 良い考えですね

C Listen and practice the role play until you can give it fluently.

 Studying further

Trying it out

Practice the conversation by using your own ideas and information.

A: We're planning to set up a mushroom mini-farm on the roof.

B: _____

（～で何をやるつもりですか）

all those mushrooms?

A: Oh, my friend who runs a restaurant wants to use them in her dishes.

B: _____ !

（いいね！）

So she'll have fresh mushrooms all the time.

Reviewing

Fill in the blanks by referring to the definitions.

1. A material like cloth; the main structure of something

(f _ _ _ _ _)

2. A protective container

(p _ _)

3. A box or container; something that comes in a box

(p _ _ _ _ _ _)

UNIT 5

Origami Space Technology Combines Art, Design, Science

日本の伝統芸が NASA で大活躍

 ## Warming up

- ☑ 「折り紙」は英語で何というか調べてみよう

  _____

- ☑ 折り紙技術の活用事例を調べてみよう

  _____

 ## Understanding technical expressions

🎵 Disk1-26, 27

A. Match the English words with the Japanese words.

1. ( ) design		**a.** 展開する
2. ( ) deploy		**b.** 構造物
3. ( ) structure		**c.** 拡大する
4. ( ) magnify		**d.** 望遠鏡
5. ( ) telescope		**e.** 設計する

B. Look at the photo above, and then listen and complete each sentence.

1. NASA ( ) are using ideas from *origami* on a project ( ) Starshade.

（NASA の研究者たちは、Starshade と呼ばれるプロジェクトに、折り紙由来の発想を利用している）

2. Once a rocket reaches the ( ) point in space, the Starshade opens like a flower.

（ロケットが宇宙の適切な位置に到達したら、Starshade は花のように開く）

Reading Disk1-28

Since he was eight years old, Robert Salazar has been making artistic creations from folded paper. Now, he is taking his love of *origami* to a different place: outer space.

Salazar works with the Jet Propulsion Laboratory of
5 the United States space agency NASA. He says that ideas from *origami* can help design devices for research and exploration:

"*Origami* offers the potential to take a very large structure, even a vast structure, and you can get it to fit
10 within the rocket, go up, then deploy it back again. So it greatly magnifies what we are capable of building in space."

Researchers are using ideas from *origami* on several space agency projects. Manan Arya is a technologist at
15 the Jet Propulsion Laboratory. He is working on a project called Starshade. The project's goal is to fit a large object into a rocket. Once the rocket reaches the correct point in space, the Starshade opens like a flower. This large flower shape is meant to block light to permit a space telescope
20 to better see areas close to bright stars.

Starshade, Arya says, can be used to look for planets that orbit other stars. "Seeing an exoplanet next to its parent star is like trying to image a firefly next to a search light, the searchlight being the star. Starshade seeks to
25 block out that starlight so you can image a really faint exoplanet right next to it."

Researchers are also using ideas from *origami* to design a robot and a special antenna for satellites. The robot is called the Pop-up Flat Folding Explorer Robot, or
30 PUFFER.

It can fold itself flat to get into small spaces. Salazar says the robot can explore environments "otherwise inaccessible" to a robot. Antennas on satellites capture and send communications signals. Arya says it is also

artistic creation 「芸術的作品」 **fold**…「〜を折りたたむ」
outer space 「宇宙空間」

exploration 「探査」

close to…「〜に接近した」

orbit…「〜を周回する」 **exoplanet** 「太陽系外惑星」
image…「〜を撮影する」 **firefly** 「蛍」
faint 「かすかな光の」

inaccessible 「近付けない」 **capture**…「〜を捉える」

35 very useful to be able to fit large antennas into a small
space: "The bigger the antenna you have, the more gain
your antenna has."

NASA's *origami*-based technologies have a graceful

graceful 「優美な」

beauty. In *origami*, Salazar said, art, science and
40 engineering only have small differences.

Taking notes

Read the passage and take notes in Japanese.

1. 折り紙技術はどんなことに役立っているか

_____

_____

_____

2. "Otherwise inaccessible" とはどういう意味か

_____

_____

_____

Checking your comprehension

Read the passage and answer the following questions.

1. What is the purpose of the Starshade project?
   a. To minimize a rocket
   b. To house a very large structure into a rocket
   c. To see a parent star more clearly
   d. To send a rocket to the correct point in space

2. What is the purpose of the PUFFER project?
   a. To make a robot which can be folded up automatically and compactly
   b. To fit large antennas into a narrow space
   c. To make a robot which can fold paper skillfully
   d. To incorporate *origami*-based technology into science education

Accepting the challenge

1 **Practicing pronunciation**  Disk1-29, 30

A “t” は語頭にきたり、アクセントのある母音の前にくると破裂音になりますが、語尾にきた場合は、舌先は /t/ の位置に付けたままで息を解放しないので音が聞こえないことがあります。以下の音声を聴き発音してみましょう。

trash   technology   art   product   project

B 「名詞＋of」のリンキングの練習をします。以下は「折り紙」の定義文です。スムーズに言えるまで発音してみましょう。最初の「名詞＋of」は音がつながりますが、2 番目の of は母音同士なので音はつながりません。

“Origami” is the traditional Japanese art or technique of folding paper into a variety of forms such as cranes.

2 **Talking about it** Disk1-31

| Plan | Do | Check | Action |

まとめ

Stage target focus: **Planning a new product using *origami*-based technology**

 Japanese student A   Japanese student B   Student from overseas

: In this project, 1.(　　　　　) (　　　　　) (　　　　　) (　　　　　) (　　　　　) a disposable trash box by using *origami*-based technology.

: 2.(　　　　　) (　　　　　) (　　　　　) (　　　　　) (　　　　　) “origami”?

: “Origami” is the traditional Japanese technique of folding paper into a variety of forms such as cranes.

: 3.(　　　　　), (　　　　　) (　　　　　). I've seen strings of a thousand folded paper cranes.

: Now, does everybody understand the project? First we'll 4.(　　　　　) (　　　　　) (　　　　　) information about the needs of the users. After that, we'll

28

work on designing the product.

 : OK, so shall we start by thinking about the questionnaire
5.(   )?

Notes: disposable trash box「使い捨てゴミ箱」 questionnaire「アンケート」

A   Listen and complete the conversation.

B   Practice the role play until you can give it fluently.

Studying further

Trying it out

Practice the conversation by using your own ideas and information.

A: If you have a robot which can fold itself flat to get into small spaces, where would you want to use it?

B: Can it be used in inaccessible places?

A: _____ _____.

B: Well, then, I would use it for _____

_____

_____.

A: Oh, that's a good idea.

Reviewing

Fill in the blanks by referring to the definitions.

1. To open up and spread out the parts of (something, such as a parachute)

(d _ _ _ _ _)

2. A planet that orbits a star outside the solar system

(e _ _ _ _ _ _ _ _)

3. Difficult or impossible to reach, approach, or understand

(i _ _ _ _ _ _ _ _ _ _)

Toyota Plans to Offer a Robotic Leg to Help the Disabled

ロボットが高齢社会をアシスト

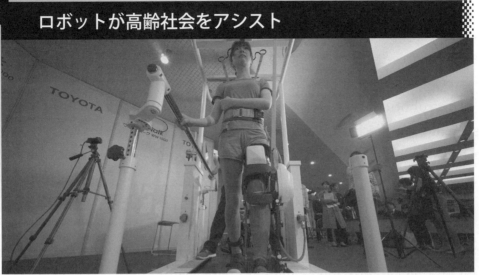

Warming up

- ☑ アシストロボットとは
  _____
- ☑ どのような分野でアシストロボットが利用されているか
  _____

Understanding technical expressions

 Disk1-32, 33

A. Match the English words with the Japanese words.

1. ( ) demonstrate	**a.** 曲げる
2. ( ) fit onto	**b.** 確保する/安全にする
3. ( ) ensure	**c.** 実演する
4. ( ) bend	**d.** 装着させる
5. ( ) straighten	**e.** まっすぐにする

B. Look at the photo above, and then listen and complete each sentence.

1. Toyota's robotic leg brace (   ) (   )
   (   ) help partially paralyzed people walk.
   (トヨタのロボット脚ギブスは半身不随の人の歩行を手助けするように設計されている)

2. The device (   ) (   ) (   )
   (   ) medical centers in Japan.
   (その装置は日本の医療センターで利用されている)

Japanese carmaker Toyota has designed a robotic leg to help disabled people walk. The company demonstrated the new device to reporters at its headquarters in Tokyo this week.

headquarters「本社」

5 The robotic leg is called the Welwalk WW-1000 system. It has a mechanical frame that fits onto a person's leg below the knee. Patients can practice walking on a special treadmill.

Eiichi Saito is a doctor and an executive vice president

executive vice president「副学長」

10 at Fujita Health University. His university helped Toyota develop the robotic leg. Saito said it is designed to be worn on one leg for patients who are paralyzed on one

paralyze…「～を麻痺させる」

side of their body because of a stroke or other disease.

The device is attached with a strap to the thigh,

thigh「大腿部」

15 knee, ankle and foot of the person using it. A motor

ankle「足首」

helps to bend and straighten the knee. Sensors provide information about what is happening and medical staff can control the system through a touch panel screen.

Toyota's Welwalk WW-1000 device uses robotic

20 technology to assist people in moving and walking. Toyota took about 10 years to develop the robot walker.

Toshiyuki Isobe, the chief officer of Toyota's Frontier

chief officer「責任者」

Research Center, told Reuters news service that it has taken the company time to develop robotics products.

25 "The biggest challenges have been in determining

challenge「難問」
determine…「～を決定する」

the needs of the robot market, which is relatively new, and to ensure that our products are safe," he said.

Robots that assist in health care are seen as an important and growing market.

30 Eiichi Saito says Toyota's device is aimed at helping people with common paralysis caused by health

paralysis「麻痺」

problems like strokes that can happen to aging people.

stroke「脳卒中」

Japan's population is aging faster than other countries. In 2015, more than 26 percent of Japanese

35 were aged 65 or older.

Some experts expect demand for robots used to assist in care of the old and disabled will increase sharply. That is because there will be fewer people in the work force to care for the growing number of older patients.

 Taking notes

Read the passage and take notes in Japanese.

1. ロボット脚の開発の手助けをした藤田保健衛生大学の才藤栄一医師によると、この装置のユーザーとして見込まれているのはどのような人か

_____

_____

_____

2. トヨタの Frontier Research Center の磯部俊之氏によると、この分野の最大の課題は何か

_____

_____

_____

Checking your comprehension

Read the passage and complete the following bullet-point summary.

Welwalk WW-1000 device is

- designed to be fitted onto _____
- attached to _____ with _____
- controlled through _____

Welwalk WW-1000 device help users

- _____
- _____ via a motor

Accepting the challenge

1 | **Practicing pronunciation**   🎧 Disk1-35, 36

A "y" は、語頭では子音 (/j/) となり、語中や語尾では母音 (/i/ /ai/) となります。特に、語頭の y が母音にならないように気をつけましょう。音声を聴き、発音してみましょう。

s**y**stem   b**y**   monthl**y**   an**y**thing   **you**   **y**es

B 子音で終わる語の後ろに、語頭が y で始まる語が続くとき、つながって音声が変化することがあります。

Woul**d y**ou like to talk with the insurance company?

2 | **Talking about it**   🎧 Disk1-37    Plan | **Do** | Check | Action

Stage target focus: **Deciding on the framework of a project**

    R&D manager

    Sales manager

🧑 : Our robotic system ¹·(   ) (   ) available for leasing to medical centers by the beginning of the next quarter.

👩 : Good. We're planning an initial one-time charge of $(①:) and a monthly rental of $(②:).

🧑 : That sounds reasonable.

👩 : ²·(   ) (   ) (   ) (   ) we need to consider?

🧑 : Well, you'd like to think about insuring the equipment, wouldn't you?

A Use the clues below and fill in the blanks ① and ② with numbers.

数字を右から３桁ごとに区切ってコンマを付けます。コンマの位置で単位を表す
単語が以下のように変わります。コンマの間は、［百の位＋（and）＋2 桁の数字］
と言う読み方をします。

1,000 → a/one thousand
1,000,000＝100 万 → a/one million
1,000,000,000＝10 億 → a/one billion
1,000,000,000,000＝1 兆→ a/one trillion

e.g. 1,756,089,153 → one billion, seven hundred (and) fifty-six million,
eighty-nine thousand, one hundred (and) fifty-three

B Referring to the Japanese below, fill in the blanks 1 and 2.

1. ねばならない
2. 他に何かあるか

C Listen and practice the role play until you can give it fluently.

 Studying further

Trying it out

Practice the conversation by using your own ideas and information.

> **A:** Wow! Did you know that more than 37,000 robots are expected to be used in healthcare over the next three years?
>
> **B:** Really, 37,000! What kind of robots?
>
> **A:** Some are for _____,
> while others are for _____
> _____.
>
> **B:** So we're going to create a healthcare robot as a new product.

Reviewing

Fill in the blanks by referring to the definitions.

1. A machine used for exercise or rehabilitation that has a large belt that moves allowing a person to walk or run on it without moving

   (t _ _ _ _ _ _ _ _)

2. Unable to move, unable to walk

   (p _ _ _ _ _ _ _ _)

3. A difficult task, something that is hard to do

   (c _ _ _ _ _ _ _ _)

Metal Recycling Businesses Prepare for More Electric Cars

ちょっと待って、捨てないで

Warming up

☑ 循環型社会の **3R** とは
_____

☑ リサイクルできるモノにどのようなものがあるか
_____

Understanding technical expressions

🎵 Disk1-38, 39

A. Match the English words with the Japanese words.

1. ( ) material	**a.** 鉱物
2. ( ) industry	**b.** 材料
3. ( ) waste metal	**c.** 回収
4. ( ) mineral	**d.** 金属くず
5. ( ) recovery	**e.** 業界

B. Look at the photo above, and then listen and complete each sentence.

1. An electric car is (　　　　　　) (　　　　　　　　) in a Paris street in France.

（電気自動車が、フランスのパリの通りで充電されている）

2. Lithium, graphite and cobalt are (　　　　　　　) (　　　　　　)
used for (　　　　　　) of electric cars.

（リチウム、グラファイト、コバルトは電気自動車のバッテリーに使用される希少金属である）

37

 **Reading** Disk1-40

Recycling businesses are improving processes to remove metals from old batteries. Their hope is to take advantage of an expected shortage of materials, such as cobalt and lithium, when sales of electric cars start rising.
5 The main problem that companies face now is a shortage of used batteries to recycle. But leaders of the recycling industry are sure that the supply, and profits, will come.

Albrecht Melber is co-managing director of the German recycling company Accurec. "The value of
10 lithium carbonate and natural and synthetic graphite has doubled or tripled in the last three or four years, becoming the most valuable materials besides cobalt in the automotive battery. There are big values that can be recycled in the future," he told the Reuters news agency.

15 Automobile manufacturers currently sell less than one million electric-powered vehicles every year. However, some experts expect electric vehicle sales to pass 14 million a year by 2025.

Larry Reaugh is head of American Manganese, a
20 Canadian recycler of metals. He notes that large lithium cobalt batteries contain high amounts of valuable minerals. "If this equated to mining, you would have a very high-grade feedstock," he said. "We're mining batteries, you might say."

However, business leaders are concerned about
25 having enough lithium for use in batteries.

Most recyclers heat old batteries to high temperatures to recover metals, a process known as pyrometallurgy. But this generally only produces cobalt, and sometimes nickel, while lithium is more difficult and costly to collect.
30 New technology is helping to recover more waste metal from used batteries. Some companies, such as Umicore, a Belgian materials technology company, say they have developed ways to get lithium once more spent, or used batteries are available for recycling.

remove…「～を取り出す」 take advantage of…「～を利用する」

profit「利益」

co-managing director「共同最高経営責任者」

lithium carbonate「炭酸リチウム」
synthetic「人造の」
besides…「～に加えて」

currently「現在」

equate to…「～に匹敵する」 mining「採掘場」
feedstock「原材料」

recover…「～を回収する」 pyrometallurgy「乾式冶金」

38

35   Umicore says it expects volumes of spent batteries to rise above 100,000 tons a year over the next 10 years, with "massive volumes" coming onto the market around 2025.

    Once that happens, the chances for the recycling
40 industry to capitalize will take off.

capitalize「乗じる」

Taking notes

Read the passage and take notes in Japanese.
    1. リサイクル業界が現在取り組んでいることは

_____

_____

    2. 電気自動車の売り上げは 2025 年までに何倍以上になることが見込まれているか

_____

Checking your comprehension

Read the passage and complete the following table in Japanese.

社名	どこの国の企業	関係者の発言の概要
Accurec		
American Manganese		
Umicore		

Accepting the challenge

1 Practicing pronunciation  Disk1-41, 42

A /b/ は発音するときに、両唇を閉じてからパッと息を出す音ですが、/v/ は上の歯を下唇に軽く当てて「ウ」という音を出しながら発音します。音声を聴き発音してみましょう。

battery o**v**er **v**olume **b**ecause **v**ehicle

B 一つの意味の塊を表す語句の、前の単語の語尾と次の単語の語頭の発音について、口の形や舌の位置が近い時に、しばしば前の単語の発音が消えてしまったように聞こえることがあります。以下の文章を下線部に気を付けて発音してみましょう。

We predict that there will be more than 100,000 tons of spent batteries to recycle over the next decade.

2 Talking about it Disk1-43

Plan **Do** Check Action

Stage target focus: **Clarifying detailed information concerning the project**

 Researcher

 News reporter

: We predict that there will be more than 100,000 tons of spent batteries to recycle over the next decade.

: How much ¹·(   ) (   ) (   )
they are expected to be? A thousand tons?

: No, a 100,000 tons!

: Wow! Can you deal with that volume?

: ²·(   ) (   ) (   ), _____
_____
_____.

A Rearrange the phrases in the parentheses, and fill in the underlined part.

(we expect there / to be / because / by 2025 / more than 14 million electric vehicles)

B Referring to the Japanese below, fill in the blanks 1 and 2.

1. 〜って言いましたか
2. 我々はしなければならないでしょう

C Listen and practice the role play until you can give it fluently.

 Studying further

Trying it out

Practice the conversation by using your own ideas and information.

> **A:** This company predicts that the auto industry will need an extra 30,000 tons of cobalt and 81,000 tons of lithium a year by 2021.
>
> **B:** Can they get that only from mining for _____ _____ ?
>
> **A:** No. They plan to also recover the minerals from _____ _____, but I'm not sure if they have the technology to do that yet.
>
> **B:** I've heard they are working on it.

Reviewing

Fill in the blanks by referring to the definitions.

1. Unprocessed material to supply or fuel a machine or industrial process

   (f _ _ _ _ _ _ _)

2. Total amount

   (v _ _ _ _ _)

3. To sell (something valuable, such as property or stock) in order to get money; to convert (something) into capital

   (c _ _ _ _ _ _ _ _)

Smart Cameras to Help You Capture Better Photos

進化するカメラ

⬧ Warming up

☑ 機械学習とは

_____

☑ 機械学習機能を取り入れた製品を考えて見よう

_____

⬧ Understanding technical expressions

 Disk1-44, 45

A. Match the English words with the Japanese words.

1. (	) weigh	**a.**	撮影する
2. (	) operate	**b.**	可能にさせる
3. (	) search	**c.**	操作する
4. (	) capture	**d.**	検索する
5. (	) allow for	**e.**	重さがある

B. Look at the photo above, and then listen and complete each sentence.

1. He is talking about the Google Clips (　　　　　) (　　　　　)
   at a Google event.
   (彼は、ハイテクカメラの Google Clips について、Google 社のイベントで話
   している)

2. Google Clips is one of the latest products to (　　　　　) (　　　　　).
   (Google Clips は、発売予定の最新の製品の一つである)

Reading Disk1-46

One of the newest "smart" devices is an old favorite, a camera. And smart cameras are getting smarter all the time.

Some are now built with machine learning tools
5 to help them think for themselves. Machine learning involves putting large amounts of data into a computer for processing. The computer uses an algorithm to process the data and learn from it. The machine then trains itself over time to make predictions and decisions
10 about future actions.

This technology helps cameras operate on their own by reacting to people and objects in a particular environment.

Google Clips is the first camera developed by the
15 web search giant that is not built into a phone. Google Clips is very small, weighing just 60 grams. The device is designed to be put somewhere in a room to take pictures by itself. It can also be attached to an object or a person's clothing.

20 Google says machine learning helps the camera choose the best times and situations for taking pictures and video clips. It can also recognize the faces of people or pets chosen by the user and take pictures of them in a more natural way.

25 Google says privacy controls have been built into the camera to give users complete control over which images they send to other devices or share with others.

The price for Google Clips is $249. The device is not yet being sold, but interested buyers can join a waiting
30 list to be informed when it is available.

GoPro is another company developing machine learning technology. The company's Hero5 and Hero6 models are designed to be easily taken anywhere and can automatically capture photos and video. The Hero5

favorite「人気者」

algorithm「アルゴリズム」

over time「時間をかけて」

search「検索」be built into…「～に搭載されている」

clothing「衣類」

control「管理機能」

waiting list「順番待ちリスト」

35   Session camera can be controlled by voice to allow for total hands-free usage. GoPro also uses machine learning to power its QuikStories feature. This tool takes existing photos and videos and automatically creates a finished video piece, complete with music and effects.

feature「機能」
existing「既存の」

complete with…「～を備えた」

40   Messaging app Snapchat sells a pair of sunglasses with a built-in camera that can record short video clips with the push of a button. Snap Inc. says the product, called Spectacles, is designed to "capture the moment, without taking you out of it."

built-in「内蔵の」

Taking notes

Read the passage and take notes in Japanese.

   1. ハイテクカメラ Hero5 Session の機能は

_____

_____

_____

   2. ハイテクカメラ Spectacles の機能は

_____

_____

Checking your comprehension

Sum up the features of Google Clips in Japanese

重さ	
ウェアラブル仕様	
機械学習機能	
プライバシー管理機能	
価格	

Accepting the challenge

A 英語の /n/ は、舌を前歯の根本にくっつけ、息を口から出さないで、鼻から出して発音します。特に語尾のｎを発音するとき、のどの奥の方で発音する日本語の「ん」にならないように気を付けましょう。音声を聞き発音してみましょう。

portio**n**   i**n**   perso**n**   ca**n**   ha**n**dle   **n**ew

B 単語中でアクセントがない母音は、舌をゆるめて「ア」と「ウ」の中間のようなあいまいな弱母音 /ə/ になります。また、文中で強勢が来ない場合、一語だけで発音する場合と発音が変わってしまう場合があります。例えば to は一語だけだと /tuː/ と発音されますが、文中では /tə/ になります。次の文を読んでみましょう。

Good teamwork is going t<u>o</u> be very import<u>a</u>nt f<u>o</u>r the s<u>u</u>ccess <u>o</u>f this project.

2 **Talking about it** Disk1-49

Plan	**Do**	Check	Action

Stage target focus: **Allotting responsibility in the project**

 Project leader

 Project member (Kaoru)

 : Good teamwork is going to be very important for the success of this project. [1](   ) (   ) (   ) (   ) tell me what portion you would like to handle?

 : [2](   ) (   ) (   ) (   ) doing the marketing research for the new product.

 : Thank you, Kaoru. I think you'd be the _____ for the job.

 : I'll get started right away.

A Fill in the underlined part by choosing a proper phrase.

ideal person   good teamwork   useful human resources

B Referring to the Japanese below, fill in the underlined parts 1 and 2.

1. ～をやりたいですか

2. ～に興味があります

C Listen and practice the role play until you can give it fluently.

 Studying further

 Trying it out

Practice the conversation by using your own ideas and information.

    A: I'll be in charge of keeping the minutes of a next meeting with clients.

    B: Why don't you use this camera _____

_____. It can be attached to your collar.

    A: What for?

    B: Well, it can automatically record the meeting so that _____

_____.

Reviewing

Fill in the blanks by referring to the definitions.

    1. Set of steps that are followed in order to solve a mathematical problem

(a _ _ _ _ _ _ _ _)

    2. Allowing something to work or happen without being directly guided

(a _ _ _ _ _ _ _ _ _ _ _ _)

    3. A computer program that performs an activity

(a _ _)

UNIT 9 Scientists Uncover Mystery of Mosquito Flight

敵を知れば百戦殆からず

Warming up

- ☑ 蚊のどんな特徴が人間にとって害になるか

- ☑ 蚊の飛び方にはどんな特徴があるか

Understanding technical expressions

CD Disk1-50, 51

A. Match the English words with the Japanese words.

1. (　　) disease	**a.** 昆虫
2. (　　) insect	**b.** 力学
3. (　　) mechanics	**c.** 触角
4. (　　) view	**d.** 病気
5. (　　) antenna	**e.** 画像データ

B. Look at the photo above, and then listen and complete each sentence.

1. The Anopheles gambiae mosquito (　　　　　　　) the malaria parasite.

（ガンビアハマダラカ（写真の蚊）はマラリア原虫をまき散らす）

2. A mosquito has two antennae, or tall, thin (　　　　　　　) on its head.

（蚊には、2本の触角、すなわち長くて細い器官が頭の上にある）

49

The mosquito is a troublesome and sometimes dangerous insect. Their bites itch and can carry dangerous diseases, like malaria, Zika virus and yellow fever.

Recently, researchers from Britain and Japan discovered how mosquitoes fly. This knowledge, they say, will help find ways to stop mosquitoes from spreading diseases in the future.

Mosquito wings are small and have an uncommon shape. Because of this, it is hard to believe that they are able to fly. So, how is their flight possible?

The team of scientists from Britain and Japan solved the mystery. They used high-speed cameras and computer images to understand the mechanics of how the insect moves its wings to stay in the air. Researchers at the University of Oxford took images of mosquito wing movements. They set up eight super-high speed cameras that take 10,000 images each second.

Simon Walker is a researcher at the University of Oxford.

"So normally to record an insect you need at least two cameras, ideally more, so you've got enough views of an insect because with two camera views you can then take any point on an insect and calculate its 3-D coordinates."

A mosquito has two antennae, or tall, thin organs on its head that it uses to feel things. But its antennae and six legs make it difficult to take clear images of the wing movements. So, the team needed to use eight cameras to view the wings from many directions.

The extra cameras let the researchers see that the mosquito's wings move eight hundred times each second. That is four times faster than many insects of a similar size.

Mosquitoes fly by moving their wings in several

bite「噛まれた跡」
itch「かゆい」
Zika virus
「ジカウィルス」

uncommon「珍しい」

coordinate「座標」

35 different directions. The thin top edges of their wings
move forward first and then they reverse direction and
move down. The movement looks almost as if the wings
are drawing the number eight.

    These researchers say that, more importantly,
40 understanding how mosquitoes fly might help find ways
to stop them from spreading diseases.

reverse「逆の」

 Taking notes

Read the passage and take notes in Japanese.

1. 蚊が媒介する伝染病にどんなものがあるか

_____

2. 日英の学者が蚊の飛び方を研究した理由は

_____

_____

 Checking your comprehension

Read the passage and answer the following questions.

1. Which of the following did the team of scientists from Britain and Japan
NOT use to find out how mosquitos fly?
  a. Super-high speed cameras
  b. Knowledge of mechanics
  c. Ten thousand visual images
  d. 3-D cameras

2. Which of the following point is unique about how mosquitoes fly?
  a. Slow movements of its wings
  b. Unsteady movements of its wings
  c. Flying as if drawing the number eight
  d. Flying using eight antennae on its head

Accepting the challenge

1 **Practicing pronunciation**  Disk1-53, 54

A she と sea の発音は、カタカナで書くと「シー」と同じになってしまいます。/s/ は舌先と前歯の付け根で、/ʃ/ は舌と上あごの間で摩擦音を出します。音声を聞き発音してみましょう。

section　**s**et　**sh**ould　**s**moothly　**s**ame　**sh**ame

B 一つの意味の塊を表す語句の、前の単語の語尾と次の単語の語頭の発音が同じ場合、前の単語の語尾の音が消えて１つになります。下線部に気を付けて発音してみましょう。

So I shoul<u>d d</u>o the same with the other slats?

2 **Talking about it** Disk1-55　　　| Plan | **Do** | Check | Action |

Stage target focus: **Giving instructions to the members of a project**

 Project leader　　　　　 Project member

: After we've ¹·(　　　　　) (　　　　　　) this section, we can help with the other sections.

: OK. ²·(　　　　) (　　　　) (　　　　　)
(　　　) (　　　　) (　　　　) (　　　　　)?

: Set this piece in the groove on the base. It should fit in smoothly.

: Yes, it does. So I should do the same with the other slats?

: Yes, _____.

Notes: groove「溝」　slat「細長い板」

A Use the clues below to rearrange the phrases in parentheses, and fill in the underlined part.

プロジェクトの遂行段階になると、メンバー間で**指示文**が飛び交うようになります。**指示文**は、通常命令文の形をとります。何かを行わないように指示する場合は否定命令文が使われます。メンバーの立場によっては、丁寧な指示文が使われることもあります。

- **Make sure**… 「必ず〜してください」
- **Do not + 動詞** 「〜しないでください」
- **Would you...?** 「〜してくださいませんか」

(until / in / all slats / are / place / continue)

B Referring to the Japanese below, fill in the blanks 1 and 2.

1. 組み立てを終える
2. 私に何をして欲しいですか

C Listen and practice the role play until you can give it fluently.

 Studying further

Trying it out

Practice the conversation by using your own ideas and information.

A: We are trying to design a better drone, so let's study mosquito flight?

B: Why mosquitos?

A: Oh, _____

_____.

B: I see.

Reviewing

Fill in the blanks by referring to the definitions.

1. To have or produce an unpleasant feeling on your skin or inside your mouth, nose, etc. that makes you want to scratch

(i _ _ _)

2. A part of an animal's body that is used for flying or gliding

(w _ _ _)

3. One of a set of numbers that is used to locate a point on a map or graph

(c _ _ _ _ _ _ _ _)

Scientists Praise Developments in Smell Technology

次世代 VR の世界

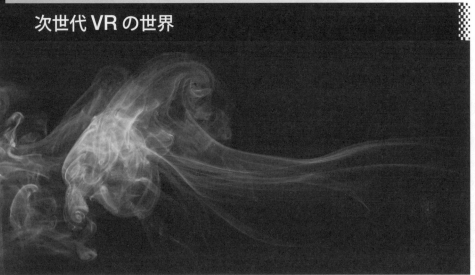

Warming up　学習の前に以下の課題について調べてみよう。

- ✓ 仮想現実（VR）とは
　_____
- ✓ 匂いの VR の例
　_____

Understanding technical expressions

 Disk1-56, 57

A. Match the English words with the Japanese words.

1. (　　　) release　　　　　**a.** 熱帯雨林
2. (　　　) rainforest　　　　**b.** 感情
3. (　　　) immersive　　　　**c.** 越える
4. (　　　) emotion　　　　　**d.** 発する
5. (　　　) exceed　　　　　**e.** 没入型の

B. Look at the photo above, and then listen and complete each sentence.

1. Researchers have created virtual reality environments that even
　(　　　　　　　) (　　　　　　　　　) the real thing.
　（研究者たちが本物と同じ匂いさえする仮想現実環境を作り出した）

2. People will soon have (　　　　　　　) (　　　　　　　)
　(　　　　　　　) (　　　　　　　　　).
　（人々は間もなく匂いの技術を使った装置を使うようになるだろう）

 **Reading** Disk1-58

Would you buy a car that released calming smells into the air when you are stuck in heavy traffic? Would you buy a robot that smells like a human being?

Scientists suggest that new technology means people
5 will soon be using devices like these in their daily lives.

The British Science Festival took place recently in Brighton, England. At the event, researchers from the University of Sussex demonstrated some of the technology that might be coming soon. Many people
10 have seen the three-dimensional computer-made environments of virtual reality, known as VR. Now these virtual worlds will not just look and sound real. Researchers have created VR environments that even smell like the real thing.

15 With the new technology, users open a virtual door and step into a new environment, like a rainforest. After they enter this virtual world, special equipment releases forest-like smells into the air to make the experience seem more real.

20 Suzanne Fisher-Murray saw the technology being demonstrated at the British Science Festival. She told VOA, "It is a really immersive experience that you have because you're exploring this environment and you have smells … with it."

25 Smell technology has been tried in the past. In the United States, Smell-O-Vision was designed to provide smells during the showing of a movie. The Smell-O-Vision system was briefly popular in the 1960s. Now, University of Sussex researcher Emanuela Maggioni says
30 it is close to becoming popular again.

"The connection with emotions, memories, and … the sense of smell," Maggioni said. "It is incredible what we can do with technology."

The uses for smell technology are not just limited

calming「気を静めるような」
be stuck in heavy traffic「渋滞に巻き込まれる」

demonstrate…「〜を披露する」

explore…「〜を探検する」

briefly「少しの間」

incredible「信じられないほど素晴らしい」

35 to films and the performing arts. Researchers also
demonstrated a computer program where users could
imagine themselves driving a car. The system included a
special smell-spraying device. Dmitrijs Dmitrenko is one
of the researchers working on this project.

work on「取り組む」

40   "In this demonstration," he said, "we wanted to
deliver the smell of lavender every time the driver

deliver…「〜を出す」

exceeds the speed limit. We chose lavender because it's a

exceed…「〜を超える」

very calming smell."

Taking notes

Read the passage and take notes in Japanese.

1. 匂い技術を使った例として冒頭で述べられているものを２つ

_____

_____

2. どこで、誰が匂いを使った技術の披露をしたのか

_____

_____

Checking your comprehension

Read the passage and answer the following questions.

1. Which of the following is given as an example of a device using smell technology?
  a. A robot releasing the smell of lavender
  b. A dog-shaped robot that smells like a dog
  c. A smell-spraying device when driving

2. Which of the following is true about Suzanne Fisher-Murray?
  a. She is one of the researchers that created 3D VR environments.
  b. She experienced a demonstration of smell technology at a science festival.
  c. She designed Smell-O-Vision system in the 1960s.

Accepting the challenge

A 動詞の単語の ing 形は /iŋ/ という発音になります。/ŋ/ は舌の後ろ部分を上げて、上あごの奥につけて息を鼻から抜いて出します。音声を聴き発音してみましょう。

develop**ing**　depend**ing**　typ**ing**　us**ing**　los**ing**

B 語句が一つの意味の塊を表すとき、前の単語の語尾が子音で、それに続く単語の語頭が母音の場合、音がつながります。以下の文章を下線部に気を付けて発音してみましょう。

This is the new device we are developing based on smell technology.

2 **Talking about it** Disk1-61

| Plan | **Do** | Check | Action |
まとめ

Stage target focus: **Developing a new product using smell technology**

 Project leader

 Researcher

 External marketing consultant

 : This is the new device we are developing based on smell technology.

 : 1.(　　　　　) (　　　　　) (　　　　　)
(　　　　　)?

 : It is meant to be placed on your office desk. It releases different smells depending on your alertness condition.

 : 2.(　　　　　) (　　　　　) (　　　　　)
(　　　　　) (　　　　　) alertness condition?

 : It has a sensor that judges your status based on your posture and your movements, for example, how quickly you are typing or using the mouse.

 : If it judges that you seem to be losing focus, it will release a citrus fragrance to raise your concentration level.

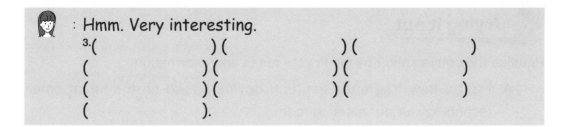

: Hmm. Very interesting.

3.(   ) (   ) (   )
 (   ) (   ) (   )
 (   ) (   ) (   )
 (   ).

A   Listen and complete the conversation.

B   Practice the role play until you can give it fluently.

Studying further

Trying it out

Practice the conversation by using your ideas and information.

> **A:** I got a new fragrance-emitting device based on the latest smell technology for our meeting room.
>
> **B:** What? What does it do?
>
> **A:** Well, it will help us _____
> _____ but will also help us _____
> _____.
>
> **B:** Really?!
>
> **A:** Yes, if you put it on your desk and set it to "meeting mode," it will send out a lemony fragrance. If you set it to "break mode," you'll smell lavender.

Reviewing

Fill in the blanks by referring to the definitions.

1. A plant with narrow leaves and small purple flowers that have a sweet smell

   (l _ _ _ _ _ _ _)

2. To go beyond the limit of something

   (e _ _ _ _ _)

3. Something, such as a message or loud sound, that tells people something is happening

   (a _ _ _ _ _ _ _)

Is a Nap after Lunch Good or Bad?

昼寝の効能とは？

 Warming up

☑ 昼寝は必要か
_____

☑ 昼寝にはどのような効果があるか
_____

 Understanding technical expressions Disk2-01, 02

A. Match the English words with the Japanese words.

1. (　　　) disorder　　　　　　**a.** 昼寝をする人
2. (　　　) napper　　　　　　　**b.** 長期の、永久の
3. (　　　) age-related　　　　　**c.** 障害
4. (　　　) permanent　　　　　 **d.** 年齢に関わる
5. (　　　) last　　　　　　　　 **e.** 続く

B. Look at the photo above, and then listen and complete each sentence.

1. She is (　　　　　　　　　) a good night's sleep.

　（彼女はぐっすり眠っているところである）

2. (　　　　　　　　　) can help brain (　　　　　　　　　) in older adults.

　（昼寝は高齢者の脳の活動を助ける）

Michael Twery is director of the National Center on Sleep Disorders Research at America's National Institutes of Health. Twery is an expert on the science of sleep and sleep disorders. He told me that a good night's sleep
5 helps to learn better.

the science of sleep 「睡眠学」

"Getting a good night's sleep is important for the learning and memory process. It's important because it stores the training exercises and the learning exercises into our more permanent memory while we're sleeping
10 7-8 hours in bed. And then the next morning when you wake up your mind is better prepared to act on that information."

But what about getting rest during the middle of the day? Short periods of sleep may help our brains work
15 better, or so says a recent study on napping.

Past studies have shown that napping can help babies and young children learn better. And napping can help brain performance in older adults.

Taking a nap may also help this group of people fight
20 off age-related memory loss.

Take China, for example. While it depends on the age and job, China, generally speaking, is a land of nappers.

So, researchers recently looked at information provided by nearly 3,000 Chinese adults, aged 65 years
25 or older. They wanted to learn if napping after a mid-day meal, a tradition in some areas, had any effect on the mental performance of the subjects.

subject「被験者」

First, the researchers asked the people if they napped and for how long. Then, based on their answers,
30 researchers put them into four groups: non-nappers (0 minutes), short nappers (less than 30 minutes), moderate nappers (30-90 minutes), and extended nappers (more than 90 minutes).

extended「長時間の」

Nearly 60 percent of those 3,000 people said they

35 did take a nap after lunch and that their naps lasted anywhere from 30 to 90 minutes. Most of the subjects who said they napped said they napped for about an hour.

   The study found that people who took an hour-long
40 nap did much better on mental tests than those who did not nap. The hour-long nappers also did better on the tests than those who napped for shorter and longer periods. In this study, it seems that the most effective nap lasted for about an hour, but not much longer.

 Taking notes

Read the passage and take notes in Japanese.

    1. 夜に良い睡眠をとるとどのような効果があるか

    _____

    _____

    2. 昼寝に関する過去の研究で分かっていることは何か

    _____

    _____

 Checking your comprehension

Read the passage and answer the following questions.

    1. What is the purpose of the recent study?
      a. To understand how taking a quick lunch can make people sleepy while working
      b. To know why taking a nap can affect the mental performance of younger people
      c. To see if napping can help brain performance in elderly people

    2. Which of the following is true about the results of the study?
      a. Almost all the 3,000 Chinese people said they took a nap after lunch.
      b. About 1,800 people said they took a 30-90-minute nap.
      c. The 1,800 people said they took a 60-minute nap.

Accepting the challenge

A 母音の発音 /iː/ /uː/ は、日本語の「イ」や「ウ」より少し舌や唇などを緊張させ
て発音します。音声を聴き発音してみましょう。

aftern**oo**n   n**ew**   s**ee**m   employ**ee**   sl**ee**p   n**ee**d   l**ea**d

B 英語の音声が聞き取れない理由は、強弱のイントネーションに慣れていないこと
と、音がつながった時の音の変化に慣れていないせいです。特に前置詞を伴う句
のつながった音の変化に慣れるよう、練習してみましょう。

<u>in the afternoon</u>   <u>with the new ones</u>   <u>in the US</u>

2 **Talking about it**    Disk2-06 | Plan | Do | **Check** | Action |

Stage target focus: **Identifying problems**

  Business executive

  Department manager
(Ms. Tanaka)

 : Ms. Tanaka, many of the employees [1]·(   )
(   ) (   ) (   )
(   ) (   ) in the afternoon.

 : Yes, I've noticed that, especially with the new ones.

 : Any suggestions on what to do?

 : Well, _____
_____. Some companies in the US allow
employees to take short naps.

 : [2]·(   ) (   ) (   )
(   ) (   ).

A Rearrange the phrases in the parentheses, and fill in the underlined part.

(need to / some serious measures / take / this / to / stop / we will)

B Referring to the Japanese below, fill in the blanks 1 and 2.

1. 士気が低いようだ

2. やってみてもいいかも知れないね

C Listen and practice the role play until you can do it fluently.

 Studying further

Trying it out

Practice the conversation by using your own ideas and information.

> **A:** Did you know that not sleeping enough can lead to sleep debt?
>
> **B:** You're kidding! I sleep only 5 hours. Maybe that's why I'm always sleepy during working hours.
>
> **A:** Oh, no. You need _____
>
> _____.
>
> **B:** Really?! Well then, I need _____
>
> _____!

Reviewing

Fill in the blanks by referring to the definitions.

1. To sleep briefly especially during the day

   (n _ _)

2. A person who is the focus of scientific or medical attention or experiment

   (s _ _ _ _ _)

3. An abnormal physical or mental condition

   (d _ _ _ _ _ _)

Smart Mirrors Show What You Would Look Like Wearing Those Earrings

進化するスマートフォンアプリ

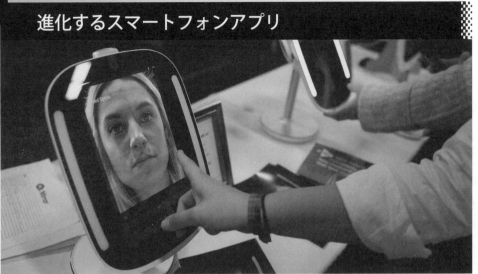

 Warming up

☑ 写真加工スマートフォン・アプリケーションとは

_____

☑ 活用事例にどのようなものがあるか

_____

 Understanding technical expressions　 Disk2-07, 08

A. Match the English words with the Japanese words.

1. ( ) mobile	**a.** 機能
2. ( ) app	**b.** 在庫（品）
3. ( ) function	**c.** 〜のように見える
4. ( ) appear	**d.** 携帯の
5. ( ) inventory	**e.** アプリケーション

B. Look at the photo above, and then listen and complete each sentence.

1. She is using a virtual (　　　　　　　).

（彼女は、バーチャル・ミラーを使っている）

2. These smart mirror applications are gaining (　　　　　　　) among
(　　　　　　　) businesses.

（このスマート・ミラー・アプリケーションは、小売店の間で人気が出ている）

67

 **Reading**   Disk2-09

Software applications let smart phone users do a lot with their photographs.

Apps such as Snapchat already give users the ability to add dog ears, colorful rainbow tongues and other
5 images onto smart phone photos.

Virtual mirrors are a little different. They are designed to let users see what they would look like wearing products that they might want to buy. Some examples are earrings or other jewelry, lipstick and eyeglasses.

10 These smart mirror applications are gaining popularity among retail businesses, which want to get people into their stores.

A smart mirror is simply an app that turns the screen of a smart phone or other mobile device into a mirror,
15 using its camera function. As users look at the image, the app will make it appear as if they are wearing the product.

Peter Johnson is with FaceCake Marketing Technologies. He said, "Virtual try-on offers people the ability to try on numerous products, many more than
20 they would be able to try on otherwise."

Recently, Johnson demonstrated how an app called Dangle works. The software program lets store customers try on different earrings without touching a single pair.

Dangle can be used on a computer tablet. It uses the
25 tablet's camera and the app's facial recognition technology to make it appear as if the user is wearing earrings.

The digital earrings in the image appear almost real. They move with the user, providing a realistic experience. With Dangle, retailers can show customers all of their
30 earrings in a short period of time — something almost impossible without technology.

There are other good reasons to use the app. Trying-on products with the virtual mirror means there is nothing to damage, lose or at risk of being stolen.

as if…「まるで〜のように」

try-on「試着」

numerous「様々な」

otherwise「別の方法で（ここでは実際に身に着けることを指す）」

at risk of...「〜の危険がある」

35   "In-store jewelry, even costume jewelry, is now quite expensive," noted Peter Johnson.

"This is a way to keep inventory secure, while people are making decisions about what they want to wear," he said.

 ## Taking notes

Read the passage and take notes in Japanese.

1. Snapchat というアプリケーションを使うと何ができるか

_____

_____

_____

2. Smart mirror とはどのようなアプリケーションか

_____

_____

_____

 ## Checking your comprehension

Read the following sentences about Dangle. Decide whether it is T(true) or F (false).

1. (   ) A software that lets people try on various clothes

2. (   ) A software program that can be used for making earrings

3. (   ) An application that allows customers to virtually try on earrings

4. (   ) An application that helps keep the store inventory secure

5. (   ) A software program that works on a computer tablet

Accepting the challenge

1 | **Practicing pronunciation**   🎧 Disk2-10, 11

A　アメリカ英語ではフラッピング（flapping）といって2つの母音の間に挟まれた /t/ の音は /r/ や /d/ に近い音として発音されます。音声を聴き発音してみましょう。

computer　　better　　pattern　　photo　　matter

B　3つの語句を and や or で結ぶ場合のイントネーションは、最初の↗2つは上昇調で読み、最後は下降調で読みます。

dog ears, ↗　colorful rainbow tongues ↗　and other images ↘

There is nothing to damage, ↗　lose ↗　or at risk of being stolen. ↘

2 | **Talking about it**   🎧 Disk2-12

| Plan | Do | **Check** | Action |

Stage target focus: **Discussing solutions**

Software engineer　　　　　　　　　Client

: I think ¹·(　　　　　) (　　　　　) (　　　　　)
(　　　　　) (　　　　　) (　　　　　) make the clothes move naturally with the wearer. What do you think?

: I think it will be making the cloth patterns move naturally.

: Yes, that will be a challenge. _____
_____ and
²·(　　　　　) (　　　　　) (　　　　) (　　　　)
(　　　　　) (　　　　　) the patterns.

A Use the clues to rearrange the phrases in the parentheses, and fill in the underlined part.

> **手順・順序を表す表現**
>
> 指示を出したり、機器の操作の仕方を説明する場合は、段階的にどのようなことをすべきなのか簡潔に伝える必要があります。その際、以下のような表現を使うと分かりやすく伝えられます。
>
> ①最初に **first / first of all**   ②次に **then / next**   ③最後に **finally**
>
> e.g.) First, put some coffee powder in the cup, and then pour some boiling water. Finally, add some sugar if you like.

(move with the wearer / how to / make the outline / need to plan / we / first,)

B Referring to the Japanese below, fill in the blanks 1 and 2.

1. 一番難しい部分は～することでしょう

2. それから～について考えることができます

C Listen and practice the role play until you can give it fluently.

 Studying further

Trying it out

Practice the conversation by using your own ideas and information.

A: You should try this new app for choosing _____

_____.

B: How does it work?

A: It shows you what you'd look like in the clothes that you pick on the site.

B: Can it show me how I'd look if I were dancing in _____

_____?

Reviewing

Fill in the blanks by referring to the definitions.

1. A list of goods on hand

(i _ _ _ _ _ _ _)

2. Anyone who pays for goods or services

(c _ _ _ _ _ _)

3. Pricey, costly

(e _ _ _ _ _ _ _)

UNIT 13

Glowing Cancer Cells Easier to Find and Remove

癌細胞を光らせる

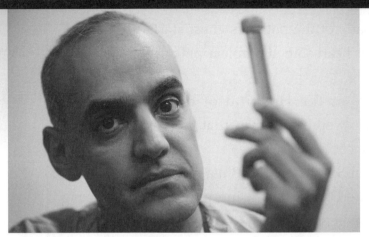

 Warming up

☑ 癌の検知法にはどのようなものがあるか

☑ どんな技術があれば、完全に癌細胞を取り除けるか考えてみよう

Understanding technical expressions

🆔 Disk2-13, 14

A. Match the English words with the Japanese words.

1. (　　) tumor   **a.** 卵巣の
2. (　　) glow   **b.** 染料
3. (　　) ovarian   **c.** 赤外線
4. (　　) dye   **d.** 光る
5. (　　) infrared light **e.** 腫瘍

B. Look at the photo above, and then listen and complete each sentence.

1. (　　　　　　　　　　) Dr. Sunil Singhal is showing a vial of
   (　　　　　　　　　　) dye.
   (外科医の Sunil Singhal 医師は蛍光色の染料のガラス瓶を見せている)

2. Using the (　　　　　　　　), doctors can easily find where cancer
   (　　　　　　　　) are in patients' bodies.
   (その染料を使うと、医師は患者の体のどこに癌細胞があるのか簡単に見つけられる)

73

The surgery looked like any other operation to remove a tumor. When doctors turned off the lights, however, parts of the patient's chest started to glow. A spot over his heart shined purplish-pink. Another spot lit
5 up in his lung.

Doctors at the Hospital of the University of Pennsylvania were using dyes that glow in the dark to help find cancer.

Dr. Sunil Singhal at the Philadelphia hospital told
10 the Associated Press that using glowing dyes is a big aid during surgery. "We can be sure we're not taking too much tissue or too little," he said.

The new dyes are experimental. There are several long-term studies that are aimed at getting the approval
15 of the Food and Drug Administration.

The drug company Johnson & Johnson recently invested $40 million in a method that uses one of the dyes. Money from the federal government also has supported some of the work.

20 Paula Jacobs, an imaging expert with the National Cancer Institute, said the new dyes will improve patients' lives. She predicts that many dyes will be available within five years.

The dye used in one of the experiments is called ICG.
25 It has been used for medical purposes for a long time.

Singhal found that when large amounts of the dye were put into the blood of a patient before surgery it would collect in cancer cells. When the cells are exposed to infrared light, they glow.

30 He calls the dye TumorGlow. Singhal has been testing it for lung, brain and other kinds of tumors.

Singhal also is testing a dye for On Target Laboratories based in the state of Indiana. The dye binds

the federal government「政府」

imaging expert「画像の専門家」

be exposed to…「～を当てる」

to a kind of protein that is common in cancer cells. It is
35 being tested on ovarian cancer and lung cancer.

In one study, the dye showed 56 of 59 lung cancers
that had been detected before surgery. The dye also
showed nine additional cancers that were not found
before surgery.

 ## Taking notes

Read the passage and take notes in Japanese.

1. ICG とは何か

_____

_____

_____

2. 染料で癌細胞が分かるのはなぜか

_____

_____

_____

 ## Checking your comprehension

Read the passage and answer the following questions.

1. What advantages of using the dye are there for doctors doing operations?
  a. They can be sure they are not removing too much tissue.
  b. It allows them to know how much tissue they should dye.
  c. This makes it possible to know how quickly they should remove cancer
     tissue.
  d. It enables them to use different colors for different cancers.

2. How do doctors use the dye for patients?
  a. They paste it directly onto the patient's body.
  b. They inject it into cancer cells.
  c. They inject it into the patient's blood.
  d. They put it into the patient's cancerous organs.

Accepting the challenge

1 **Practicing pronunciation**  Disk2-16, 17

A 母音 /e/ /æ/ を発音する時の口の形は似ています。/æ/ は日本語の「え」の唇の形を少し横に広げて「あ」の音を出します。音の違いに注意して、音声を聴き発音してみましょう。

l**a**mp s**a**mple p**a**ss inst**ea**d wavel**e**ngth g**e**t th**e**m

B 文章の中で前置詞や冠詞などは強勢が置かれないので、音がつながります。前置詞の前にある名詞の語尾と音がつながる場合もあります。音声を聴き発音してみましょう。

It uses **light of a** different wavelength.

2 **Talking about it**  Disk2-18 Plan Do **Check** Action

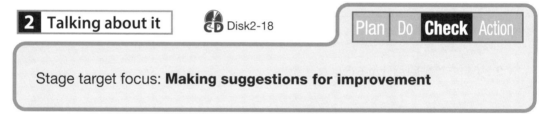

Stage target focus: **Making suggestions for improvement**

 Project leader Researcher

 : This lamp is not working as it should.

 : ¹·(   ) (   ) (   )
(   ) (   ) (   )
(   )?

 : How is it different from this one?

 : Well, it uses light of a different wavelength. _____
_____ .

 : I see. OK, ²·(   ) (   ) (   ).

A Rearrange the phrases in the parentheses, and fill in the underlined part.

(make / to see / it / might / easier / the dyes)

B Referring to the Japanese below, fill in the blanks 1 and 2.

1. 代わりにこちらのものを試してみたらどうですか
2. それを試してみましょう

C Practice the role play until you can give it fluently.

 ## Studying further

Trying it out

Practice the conversation by using your own ideas and information.

> **A:** Please pass me _____
>
> _____. These are too large for this sample.
>
> **B:** Here you are. If these don't work, there are others _____
>
> _____.
>
> **A:** Really? Could you get them for me?
>
> **B:** Sure. They're right here if you need them.

Reviewing

Fill in the blanks by referring to the definitions.

   1. A substance that changes the color of something

(d _ _)

   2. To shine with a low light

(g _ _ _)

   3. A mass of cells that are not normal

(t _ _ _ _)

Meet CIMON, a 'Floating' Space Assistant for Astronauts

宇宙に AI が行く時代

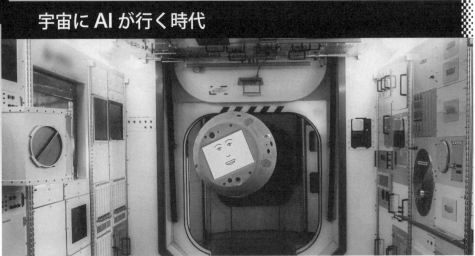

Warming up

☑ AI が搭載された機器はどんなものがあるか

☑ 宇宙ステーションのような閉塞空間で AI が活躍するのはどのような場合か

Disk2-19, 20

Understanding technical expressions

A. Match the English words with the Japanese words.

1. (   ) power
2. (   ) astronaut
3. (   ) aerospace
4. (   ) weightlessness
5. (   ) command

a. 指令
b. 宇宙飛行士
c. 無重力
d. 航空宇宙の
e. 動かす

B. Look at the photo above, and then listen and complete each sentence.

1. The (   ) assistant called CIMON will be used aboard the International Space Station (   ) a coming mission.
   (CIMON という AI が搭載されたアシスタントが次のミッションの間に国際宇宙ステーション上で使用される予定である)

2. It is a (   ) device with a computer-like display in (   ).
   (それは前面にコンピュータのような画面のついた丸い機器である)

Google Home, Amazon Echo and Apple HomePod are all artificial intelligence AI-powered systems that respond to voice commands. The systems connect to the internet to look up information, play music or movies, or
5 control household devices.

Now, researchers have developed the first AI assistant for use in space. European aerospace company Airbus cooperated with U.S.-based IBM on the system. It will be deployed to the International Space Station (ISS)
10 during a mission in June.

Airbus says it is the first time an AI system will be used aboard the ISS.

The assistant is called CIMON, which stands for Crew Interactive Mobile Companion. It is a round device
15 weighing about five kilograms. It is designed to move around by itself and follow the movements of humans. It has a computer-like display in front for showing many kinds of information.

An official from Airbus describes it as "a kind of flying
20 brain" designed to support astronauts in their daily work. The digital "brain" is powered by IBM's AI processing system called Watson.

Just like digital assistants for the home, CIMON uses AI to learn and predict human behaviors from repeated
25 interactions over time. The system is trained to recognize voices and faces so it can respond directly with people.

over time「時間をか
けて」

CIMON will be tested by German astronaut Alexander Gerst during the European Space Agency's upcoming Horizons mission aboard the ISS from June to
30 October. Gerst will command the space station during the second half of the mission.

Flight tests will be carried out before the mission to make sure CIMON operates correctly in conditions of weightlessness.

35   Gerst will perform three specific experiments with CIMON. One will examine the effects of space on crystals. He will also team up with CIMON to solve a Rubik's cube. A third medical experiment will use CIMON as a "smart" flying camera.

team up with…「～と組む」

40   The researchers say these experiments are just a start. They hope to use CIMON to interact and assist astronauts on many future missions.

Taking notes

Read the passage and take notes in Japanese.

1. 家庭で使われる AI 搭載のシステムでは、どのようなことができるか

_____

_____

_____

2. CIMON が最初の宇宙ミッションで行う 3 つの実験は何か

_____

_____

_____

Checking your comprehension

Read the passage and complete the following table in Japanese.

CIMON の仕様	
開発者	
重量	
機能	
搭載されているシステム	

Accepting the challenge

1 **Practicing pronunciation**  Disk2-22, 23

A つづり字 "y" だけでなく /j/ の音が出てくるつづり字は他にもあります。音声を聴き発音してみましょう。

unit contin**u**e **u**se n**ew** **Eu**ropean

B 文中は、強調したい場合以外は、代名詞、接続詞、前置詞、be 動詞・助動詞、冠詞には通常強勢は置かれません。弱強に気を付けてリズミカルに英文を読んでみましょう。

If this problem continues, we might need to redo the sound system.

・ ・ ● ● ・ ・ ● ・ ● ・ ● ●

2 **Talking about it** Disk2-24

| Plan | Do | **Check** | Action |

Stage target focus: **Reporting how the plan is progressing**

 Project leader

 Head of operations

: Most operations are proceeding smoothly but ¹·(   )
(   ) (   ) (   ) (   ) the new
AI unit.

: Oh, what sort of problems?

: Well, _____ sometimes.

: Have you checked the microphone unit?

: Yes, but ²·(   ) (   ) (   )
(   ) (   ) (   )
(   ). If this problem continues, we might need
to redo the sound system.

A　Use the clues to rearrange the phrases in the parentheses, and fill in the underlined part.

> **問題点を指摘する表現（プロジェクト遂行における問題点の指摘）**
> 断定はできないけれども、状況的な証拠から問題があると思われる場合、**seem to v**「〜のようである」という表現を使って、問題点を指摘することができます。
>
> *e.g.)* **The system** boxed{seems to} **fail to recognize voices and faces.**
> （システムが声と顔の認識ができていないようである）

(to / recognizing voices / seems / have trouble / it)

B　Referring to the Japanese below, fill in the blanks 1 and 2.

1. まだ〜に問題があります
2. 悪いところがあるように見えません

C　Listen and practice the role play until you can give it fluently.

Studying further

Trying it out

Practice the conversation by using your own ideas and information.

A: There seems to be a problem with _____

_____ .

B: Really, what's wrong?

A: Well, _____ .

B: I see. Let me check _____

_____ .

Reviewing

Fill in the blanks by referring to the definitions.

1. Using or related to computer technology

(d _ _ _ _ _ _)

2. The ability of a machine to reproduce human behavior

(a _ _ _ _ _ _ _ _ _ i _ _ _ _ _ _ _ _ _ _ _)

3. Electronic device (such as a computer monitor) that shows information

(d _ _ _ _ _ _)

UNIT 15 Do Bats Hold the Secret to Long Life?

コウモリが教える老化の意味

 ## Warming up

✓ 老化の原因は何か考えよう

_____

✓ 一般的に長寿の秘訣はどのようなものだろうか

_____

 ## Understanding technical expressions

 Disk2-25, 26

A. Match the English words with the Japanese words.

1. (　　) chromosome   **a.** 健康寿命
2. (　　) gene   **b.** 哺乳動物
3. (　　) molecule   **c.** 遺伝子
4. (　　) mammal   **d.** 染色体
5. (　　) health span   **e.** 分子

B. Look at the photo above, and then listen and complete each sentence.

1. European researchers are studying (　　　　　　　) to understand the secret of their long (　　　　　) (　　　　　).

   （ヨーロッパの研究者たちは、長い寿命の秘密を理解するため、コウモリの研究を行っている）

2. Scientists hope that studying bats will (　　　　　) them to learn more about the processes that drive (　　　　　) (　　　　　).

   （コウモリを研究すれば、健康的に老いるプロセスについて多くを学ぶことが出来ると科学者たちは期待している）

Bats are the only mammals that can fly a great distance, but they have another ability. Many bats live a very long time for an animal their size.

European researchers are studying bats to understand
5 why they live so long. They hope to make discoveries aimed at fighting the aging process in human beings.

The group of scientists said they had identified important biological qualities in some bat species.

The group studied bat chromosomes, a line of genes
10 found in the nucleus of cells. The scientists were most interested in structures connected to the ends of the chromosomes. They are called telomeres.

nucleus「核」

telomere「テロメア」

Telomeres protect the ends of chromosomes, which shorten each time a cell divides. Scientists believe this
15 shortening process causes cells to break down. They say this is what causes aging.

A report on bats was published in the journal *Science Advances*.

Among the leaders of the study was Emma Teeling, a
20 biologist with University College Dublin in Ireland.

Teeling said studying long-living mammals that have developed ways to fight aging "is an alternative way to identify the molecular basis of extended 'health spans.'"

extended「長い」

She added that studying bats enables scientists to
25 learn more about the processes "that drive healthy aging."

The European researchers studied 493 bats from four bat species. The group used information that had been gathered over more than 60 years.

Of these animals, the greater mouse-eared bat
30 generally lived the longest, an average of 37 years.

mouse-eared bat「ホオヒゲコウモリ」

The scientists said this and a related species, which are grouped together under the name Myotis, had telomeres that did not shorten with age. Another Myotis bat holds the record for oldest age, reaching 41 years.

Myotis「ホオヒゲコウモリ属」

35   The scientists' findings suggest that these bats' cells have the ability to maintain and repair their telomeres.

 Taking notes

Read the passage and take notes in Japanese.

　　1. テロメアとは何か

　　_____

　　_____

　　_____

　　2. テロメアは何をするものか

　　_____

　　_____

　　_____

 Checking your comprehension

Read the passage and choose the best answer for each question.

　　1. Which of the following sentences is NOT true about the purpose of the European scientists' research?

　　　a. To understand the mechanism of aging

　　　b. To find ways to extend life span

　　　c. To identify what breaks down cells

　　　d. To learn more about flying mammals

　　2. How many years did the most long-living bat on record live?

　　　a. 37　　**b.** 41　　**c.** 60　　**d.** 493

Accepting the challenge

  Disk2-28, 29

A 子音の /r/ と /l/ の発音は注意が必要です。/r/ は唇を「ウ」の形にすぼめて、舌先をどこにもつけずに発音します。一方、3 章で学習した、後に母音が続くライト L （/l/）と呼ばれるものは、舌を上歯の裏につけて「ウ」とうなってから、舌をはじくように発音します。音声を聴き発音してみましょう。

extreme   experiment   collect   revise   fly   plan

B 7 章では、前の単語の語尾と次の単語の語頭の発音について、口の形や舌の位置が近い時に、しばしば前の単語の発音が消えてしまったように聞こえることがあると学習しましたが、特に前の単語の語尾が破裂音の時に起こります。以下の文章を下線部に気を付けて発音してみましょう。

We've had trouble collecting enough specimens.
We can find some other way to get the same information.

2 **Talking about it**   Disk2-30
Plan Do **Check** Action
まとめ

Stage target focus: **Checking the process of experimental procedures using specimens**

 Project leader   Researcher

 : How are the experiments coming along?

: Overall, everything is proceeding smoothly except for the experiments with the flies.

: Oh, ¹·(   ) (   )?

: Well, because of the extreme weather conditions this year, we've had trouble collecting enough specimens.

 : I see. Then ²·(   ) (   )
(   ) (   ) (   )
(   ) (   ) to the original plans.

: Yes, what would you suggest we do?

: Well, ³·(   ) (   ) (   )
(   ) (   ) (   )
(   ) (   ) (   ) from the
fly experiments. If we can find some other way to get the
same information, we may be able to revise our plans.

 Listen and complete the conversation.

 Practice the role play until you can give it fluently.

Studying further

Trying it out

Practice the conversation by using your own ideas and information.

A: We've set up the insect traps. But, because of _____

_____

_____, we've not been able to collect as

many as we expected.

B: Hmm. That means that we won't have enough samples for all of the

experiments.

A: Yes, we may have to _____

_____.

B: I see. What would you suggest we do?

Reviewing

Fill in the blanks by referring to the definitions.

1. Animals that produce milk, have hair and have a high body
   temperature

   (m _ _ _ _ _ _)

2. Another way or possibility

   (a _ _ _ _ _ _ _ _ _)

3. To keep up or protect in an existing state

   (m _ _ _ _ _ _ _)

UNIT 16 New Battery-Free Cellphone Is Powered by Radio Signals

もう電池残量を気にしなくていい？

 **Warming up**

☑ 無線周波数とは
_____

☑ 無線周波数はどのようなものに使われているか
_____

Understanding technical expressions   🄲🄳 Disk2-31, 32

A. Match the English words with the Japanese words.

1. (　　) frequency   **a.** 飛躍
2. (　　) ambient   **b.** 周波数
3. (　　) current   **c.** 送る
4. (　　) transmit   **d.** 周囲の
5. (　　) leap   **e.** 電流

B. Look at the photo above, and then listen and complete each sentence.

1. Researchers have built a cellphone that can (　　　　　　　　)
(　　　　　　　) (　　　　　　　　) (　　　　　　　　　) without batteries.
(研究者たちがバッテリーなしに電話をかけたり受けたりできる携帯電話を作った)

2. The new phone picks up small (　　　　　　　) (　　　　　　　)
and runs on very small amounts of (　　　　　　　).
(その新しい携帯電話は小さな電気信号を拾い、ごく少量の電力で動く)

Researchers have built a cellphone that does not need batteries. They say the phone can send and receive calls using power from radio signals or light.

A team from the University of Washington in Seattle
5 is currently testing a prototype of the phone.

The researchers were able to develop a device that uses much less power than any cellphones used today. This design allows the new phone to run on very small amounts of electricity.

10 Team member Vamsi Talla says the phone picks up small electrical signals known as radio frequency, or RF waves.

"Ambient RF waves are all around us. So, as an example, your FM station broadcasts radio waves, your AM stations do that, your TV stations, your cellphone
15 towers. They all are transmitting RF waves."

broadcast「放送する、出す」

The phone can also convert ambient light into electrical current for power, according to the researchers.

convert…into~「・・・を～に変換する」

Shyam Gollakota is a professor in the Paul G. Allen School of Computer Science and Engineering. He
20 says the invention demonstrates great progress in new cellphone technology.

"This battery-free phone is a major leap in terms of the capabilities of battery-free devices. Because now we have a streaming device that can continuously talk as
25 well as receive data, which is basically a phone."

in terms of…「～に関する」

The phone identifies speech going into the microphone and coming out of the speaker. These speech vibrations are then converted into radio signals by a device called a base station.

vibration「振動」

30 The prototype has been able to operate on power gathered from radio signals from a base station up to nine meters away, according to the researchers. Using power from ambient light, it has communicated with a base station up to 15 meters away.

35   The team says the base station operating model could eventually be widely used by putting the technology in existing cellphone towers and Wi-Fi systems.

eventually「最終的には」
existing「既存の」

Taking notes

Read the passage and take notes in Japanese.

1. バッテリー不要の携帯電話は何からの電力を用いているか

_____

_____

_____

2. 基地から発せられる電波信号を利用したモデルが今後広く利用されると思われる理由は何か

_____

_____

_____

Checking your comprehension

Read the passage and answer the following questions or complete the sentence.

1. Which of the following enables the phone to have no batteries?

    a. The prototype of the phone

    b. The design of the phone

    c. FM broadcast station

    d. Conventional cellphone technology

2. Until now, the prototype of the phone has been able to

    a. operate on power from a radio station up to nine meters away.

    b. run on power from a base station nearly nine meters away.

    c. communicate with a base station up to 15 meters away using radio signals.

    d. transmit power from radio signals to a base station.

Accepting the challenge

A 疑問詞の語頭の wh の発音である /hw/ の音は「ウ」と「ワ」を同時に発音するような音です。/h/ の音が聞こえない場合もよくあります。音声を聴き練習してみましょう。

what   **wh**en   **wh**ere   **wh**ich   **wh**y

B 発音やイントネーションの矯正の訓練法にシャドーイングという方法があります。モデル音声に2単語程度遅れて、音声の残響を頼りに正確に口に出して読み上げる練習法です。音声を聴きながら以下の文章をシャドーイングしてみましょう。

It's still only a prototype, but it seems to gather power from radio signals.

2 **Talking about it** Disk2-36 | Plan | Do | Check | **Action** |

Stage target focus: **Checking the operation of the equipment**

 Project leader   Engineer

: OK, ¹·(   ) (   ) (   )
( ) the signals from the tower.

: The equipment is operating, but_____
_____.

: ²·(   ) (   ) (   ) the
receiver sensitivity?

: Ah, yes, I'm getting a strong signal now.

A Rearrange the phrases in the parentheses, and fill in the underlined part.

(signal / seem / can't / to/ get / I / any)

B Listen and complete the conversation.

1. ~をチェックすることから始めよう
2. ~を上げることできますか

C Practice the role play until you can do it fluently.

 Studying further

Trying it out

Practice the conversation by using your own ideas and information.

A: Have you seen the smartphone that can _____

_____?

B: What?! Is that possible?

A: Well, it's still only a prototype, but it seems to gather power from radio signals.

B: Wow! When will I be able to get one?

A: They should be out in _____

_____.

Reviewing

Fill in the blanks by referring to the definitions.

1. Original or first model of something from which others are developed or made

(p _ _ _ _ _ _ _)

2. Existing in the surrounding area

(a _ _ _ _ _ _)

3. Change from one thing into another

(c _ _ _ _ _ _)

Distant Star Refuses to Die

星は死ぬのか

 **Warming up**

☑ 超新星とは何か

_____

☑ 恒星は寿命がくるとどうなるか

_____

 Understanding technical expressions Disk2-37, 38

A. Match the English words with the Japanese words.

1. (　　) astronomer　　　　**a.** 観測所
2. (　　) explode　　　　　　**b.** 超新星
3. (　　) supernova　　　　　**c.** 天文学者
4. (　　) observatory　　　　**d.** 望遠鏡
5. (　　) telescope　　　　　**e.** 爆発する

B. Look at the photo above, and then listen and complete each sentence.

1. The star, officially called iPTF14hls, is a star 500 million
   (　　　　　　　　　) away from Earth.
   (正式に iPTF14hls と呼ばれている恒星は、地球から 5 億光年離れたところにある)

2. A team of scientists discovered (　　　　　　　) of a star that
   (　　　　　　　　) refuses to die.
   (科学者のあるチームが明らかに死ぬのを拒んでいる恒星の証拠を発見した)

 **Reading** Disk2-39

Scientists have long believed that a star explodes when it reaches the end of its life.

This explosion is called a supernova. NASA, the American space agency, describes a supernova as the
5 largest explosion that takes place in space.

Recently, a team of astronomers discovered evidence of one star that apparently refuses to die.

The long life of this supernova is raising questions for experts who thought they knew how dying stars worked.
10 The star, officially called iPTF14hls, is 500 million light-years away from Earth. One light-year equals 9.5 trillion kilometers.

It was found in 2014 and appeared to be a normal supernova, growing less bright over time.
15 But a few months later, astronomers at the Las Cumbres Observatory saw it getting brighter. In fact, they have seen the light grow brighter, then weaker, then stronger again five different times. They also found evidence of an explosion in the same area 60 years ago.
20 The findings were reported in the journal *Nature*.

The observatory is based in the American state of California. The astronomers say they continue to keep watch of the star with robotic telescopes around the world.

Supernovas normally grow dark after about 100 days.
25 But this one is still going strong after 1,000 days, although it is slowly getting darker.

"It's very surprising and very exciting," said Iair Arcavi, who is with the Physics Department at the University of California, Santa Barbara.
30 Arcavi led the team of astronomers. He said "We thought we've seen everything there is to see in supernova after seeing so many of them, but you always get surprised by the universe. This one just really blew away everything we thought we understood about them."

take place「起こる」

over time「時とともに」

keep watch of…「〜の観測をする」

the Physics Department「物理学部」

blow away…「〜を吹き飛ばす」

35   This supernova is believed to have once been a star up to 100 times larger than our sun. It is possibly the biggest explosion of a star ever observed. The Associated Press says this might explain its unusual ability to survive.

 ## Taking notes

Read the passage and take notes in Japanese.

1. 超新星とはどのような現象か

_____

_____

_____

2. iPTF14hls は地球からどれぐらい離れているか

_____

_____

_____

Checking your comprehension

Read the passage and complete the following table in Japanese.

	通常の超新星	iPTF14hls
明るさはどうなるか		
寿命		

Accepting the challenge

 Disk2-40, 41

A 以下は同じ舌の位置や口唇の形で発音する有声音と無声音の組み合わせ（¹/ʒ/ /ʃ/ と ²/dʒ/ /tʃ/）です。音声を聴き発音してみましょう

    1. expo**s**ure   **sh**ould   2. ima**ge**   cap**t**ure

B リピーティングは、意味単位のフレーズを聞きとり、それを繰り返す練習法です。音声を聴き、意味を頭に思い描きながらリピートするようにしてみましょう。

This new more powerful telescope / should allow us to get / better images of the supernova.

2 | **Talking about it**   Disk2-42

Plan | Do | Check | **Action**

Stage target focus: **Implementing the revised plan**

 Researcher   Assistant

: This new more powerful telescope should allow us to get better images of the supernova. _____

_____.

: ¹·(   ) (   ) (   )
(   ) (   ) use a longer exposure time this time?

: Yes, that's a good idea. ²·(   ) (   )
the exposure time (   ) (   )
(   ).

: This new equipment should then make it possible to capture more details.

A Use the clues to rearrange the phrases in the parentheses, and fill in the underlined part.

> **製品・技術を説明する頻出表現（比較級、倍数表現）**
>
> 　倍数を表す場合は、2倍は twice、3倍以上は three times、four times…という表現を使い、比較級の形容詞の前に置きます。また比較対象が不明の場合や、明らかな場合は than 以下は省略されます。
>
> This supernova is believed to have once been a star up to **100 times** <u>larger than</u> our sun.（この超新星は、かつては太陽の100倍までになった大きさの星だったと考えられている）

(the previous one / the power / greater than / is / around 10 times)

B Referring to the Japanese below, fill in the blanks 1 and 2.

1. ～すべきだと思いますか？

2. ～をもう少し長くしましょう

C Listen and practice the role play until you can give it fluently.

 Studying further

Trying it out

Practice the conversation by using your own ideas and information.

A: It seems that this supernova is getting a bit darker.

B: Really? It's been pretty bright for almost three years now.

A: Yes, but if you review _____

_____, it seems that it might be losing its brightness.

B: Let me see _____.

Reviewing

Fill in the blanks by referring to the definitions.

1. The act or an instance of exploding

(e _ _ _ _ _ _ _)

2. A building or place given over to or equipped for observation of natural phenomena (as in astronomy)

(o _ _ _ _ _ _ _ _ _)

3. A usually tubular optical instrument for viewing distant objects by means of the refraction of light rays through a lens or the reflection of light rays by a concave mirror

(t _ _ _ _ _ _ _)

UNIT 18

Coffee to Help Power London's Buses

コーヒーがロンドンを変える

 ## Warming up

☑ 大都市の環境問題にはどのようなものがあるか
_____

☑ 廃棄物を再利用した製品を考えよう
_____

 ## Understanding technical expressions

 Disk2-43, 44

A. Match the English words with the Japanese words.

1. (　　) waste   **a.** 利用されていない
2. (　　) untapped   **b.** 排出、排出物
3. (　　) biofuel   **c.** 炭素
4. (　　) emission   **d.** 廃棄物
5. (　　) carbon   **e.** バイオ燃料

B. Look at the photo above, and then listen and complete each sentence.

1. Waste coffee (　　　　　　　　　) will be used to help fuel part of London's transportation system.

（廃棄物のコーヒーかすが、ロンドンの交通システムの燃料の一部になるよう利用されるだろう）

2. The government agency Transport for London has been turning to (　　　　　　) (　　　　　　) to cut (　　　　　　) (　　　　　　).

（地方行政機関であるロンドン交通局は、二酸化炭素の排出量を削減するために代替燃料に切り替えてきた）

Britain has long been known for its love of tea, but people in London also drink a lot of coffee.

In fact, the average Londoner reportedly drinks 2.3 cups of coffee every day.

5 And now, waste coffee grounds will be used to help fuel part of the city's transportation system.

A technology company announced on Monday that some buses will be using a biofuel that contains coffee oil.

10 The company, Bio-bean, and its partner, Argent Energy, say they have made enough coffee oil to power one of London's famous double-decker buses for a year.

The announcement made Bio-bean a trending story on social media.

15 The government agency Transport for London has been turning to biofuels to cut production of carbon emissions. A carbon emission is a gas produced by the burning of carbon. The gas is released into the atmosphere.

20 London's mayor, Sadiq Khan, said last month that his city has a "health crisis....caused directly by poor-quality air." The government has taken steps to discourage people from driving cars that do not meet European Union emissions requirements.

25 Bio-bean said Londoners produce over 200,000 tons of coffee ground waste a year. The company said it collects waste grounds from chain coffee shops and factories. The grounds are dried and processed to remove the coffee oil.

30 Bio-bean's founder Arthur Kay said, "It's a great example of what can be done when we start to reimagine waste as an untapped resource."

The coffee fuel technology has received support from the oil company Royal Dutch Shell.

partner「提携会社」

double-decker「二階建ての」
trending story「人気の話題」

crisis「危機」

requirement「要件」

reimagine…「〜をあらたに認識する」
resource「資源」

Taking notes

Read the passage and take notes in Japanese.

1. Bio-bean 社と Argent Energy 社が生産したコーヒー油の量はどれくらいか

_____

_____

_____

2. Bio-bean 社はどのようにして原料を集めてコーヒー油を生産しているか

_____

_____

_____

Checking your comprehension

Read the passage and answer the following questions.

1. What is the serious problem that London has?

  a. The amount of waste

  b. The health problem caused by poor-quality air

  c. The health crisis caused by too many buses

  d. Coffee grounds produced by chain coffee shops

2. Why have they decided to use waste coffee grounds?

  a. Londoners drink a lot of coffee.

  b. Argent Energy can cut carbon emissions.

  c. Royal Dutch Shell can support their activities.

  d. Bio-bean has already produced coffee oil.

Accepting the challenge

1 **Practicing pronunciation**  Disk2-46, 47

A 英語にはつづりと発音が相違する語はたくさんあります。母音 /au//ou/ を含む
単語に気をつけて、音声を聴き発音してみましょう。

p**ow**er   kn**ow**   gr**ou**nd   ar**ou**nd   s**o**cial   ann**ou**nce

B 長い英文を読む場合は、自分で意味の区切りを見つけて読む必要があります。意
味の区切り目に "/" （スラッシュ）を入れて、発音してみましょう。

Coffee beans have natural oils and they've developed a technology to get
that oil from used coffee grounds.

2 **Talking about it**  Disk2-48

| Plan | Do | Check | **Action** |

Stage target focus: **Testing the revised plan**

 Researcher A   Researcher B

 : ¹·(   ) (   ) this batch of oil for a
longer drive.

: Yes, ²·(   ) (   ) (   ) it
is enough to power a car for a drive around the city.

: The tests around the laboratory grounds have been
successful so far.

: Yes, but _____.

A Use the clues to rearrange the phrases in the parentheses, and fill in the underlined part.

因果関係を説明する動詞

because を使った節で原因・結果を表す文章の他に、無生物主語を使って簡潔に表す方法もあります。

A	cause	B	「A が B を引き起こす」
A	lead to	B	「A が B につながる」
A	require	B	「A のために B が必要になる」

e.g.) Some technical failures may **cause** serious problems of the system.

（いくつかの技術的な欠陥がシステムの深刻な問題を引き起こすかも知れない）

(extra power / the heavy / require / city traffic / may)

B Referring to the Japanese below, fill in the blanks 1 and 2.

1. 〜をテストしてみましょう

2. 〜かどうか見てみましょう

C Listen and practice the role play until you can do it fluently.

 Studying further

Trying it out

Practice the conversation by using your own ideas and information.

A: Say, did you know that they are planning to use coffee bean oil as biofuel for _____.

B: Coffee bean oil? I didn't know coffee beans had oil in them.

A: Oh, coffee beans have natural oils and they've developed a technology to get that oil from used coffee grounds.

B: That's great. Should I start _____
_____?

Reviewing

Fill in the blanks by referring to the definitions.

1. Something sent out or given off

(e _ _ _ _ _ _)

2. A group of businesses (such as stores, restaurants, or hotels) that have the same name and basic appearance and sell the same products or services

(c _ _ _ _)

3. Available but not used

(u _ _ _ _ _ _ _)

UNIT 19

British Start-Up Uses Feathers to Make Building Materials

驚異の天然材料

 Warming up

☑ 通常の断熱材には、どのようなものがあるか
___

☑ どのような天然材料を使った断熱材があるかを考えよう
___

 Understanding technical expressions

A. Match the English words with the Japanese words. Disk2-49, 50

1. (　　) poultry   **a.** 寄せつけない
2. (　　) biodegradable   **b.** 微生物によって分解できる
3. (　　) thermally   **c.** 家禽
4. (　　) insulation   **d.** 断熱材
5. (　　) repellent   **e.** 熱において

B. Look at the photo above, and then listen and complete each sentence.

1. Manufacturers often use bird feathers because of their (　　　　　　　　)
   (　　　　　　　) and the (　　　　　　　) they provide in a cold room
   or climate.
   (製造業者はしばしば、軽さと寒い部屋や気候の中でそれらが提供するあたたか
   さゆえに鳥の羽毛を利用する)

2. Two students from Imperial College London wanted to turn feathers
   into something (　　　　　　　　).
   (Imperial College London の 2 人の学生が、羽毛を有効活用したいと考えた)

Bird feathers have long been used in clothing and in bedding.

Manufacturers often use feathers because of their light weight and the warmth they provide in a cold room 5 or climate.

Now, two students in Britain are studying how to use them in other ways, like keeping homes warm, for example.

Chicken is a popular food in many countries, and the 10 number of poultry killed for their meat is rising.

Britain alone processes more than 945 million white-feathered chickens every year, creating tons of leftover feathers.

Two students from Imperial College London want to 15 turn these feathers into something useful.

Elena Dieckman and Ryan Robinson are each working toward a Doctor of Philosophy degree, or PhD. They are the founders of a start-up company called Aeropowder.

20 The two had an idea to create useful materials from waste. They developed a biodegradable product that could replace man-made insulation. Biodegradable materials are capable of being slowly broken down through natural processes.

25 Builders usually add insulation to homes and offices. The insulation can reduce the energy demands of heating and cooling systems.

Dieckman and Robinson won several awards for their prototype insulation, including the Mayor of London's 30 Low Carbon Entrepreneur Challenge. The $23,000 they won in the competition helped them start their company, Aeropowder.

Elena Dieckman explains why feathers are a useful material:

closing「衣料」
bedding「寝具」

leftover「残りの」

founder「創設者」
start-up company「ベンチャー企業」

35   "Feathers are a real wonder material. They are designed by nature to protect birds from really harsh environments. So they are super lightweight, they're thermally insulating, they're water-repellent, bio-degradable. So it's a really great material."

40   Robinson adds that their goal is to develop ways to use the entire feather, not just parts of it. If successful, Aeropowder may help prevent the waste of this useful natural material.

 Taking notes

Read the passage and take notes in Japanese.

1. 年間の英国で加工処理される鶏の数はどれくらいか

_____

_____

_____

2. 家を建てる際に断熱材を利用する利点は何か

_____

_____

_____

 Checking your comprehension

Read the passage and complete the following table in Japanese.

Aeropowder 社	
創設者	
受賞歴	
開発した製品	

Accepting the challenge

A 母音 /ei/ に気をつけて、音声を聴き発音してみましょう。

gr**ea**t **a**ble degr**a**dable repl**a**ce c**a**pable n**a**ture

B 発音が異なれば何を言いたいかは相手に伝わりません。分からない読み方の単語は辞書で発音を調べておく必要があります。以下の下線部の発音を調べ、読んでみましょう。

<u>Biodegradable</u> materials are capable of being slowly broken down through natural processes.

2 **Talking about it** Disk2-54

| Plan | Do | Check | **Action** |

Stage target focus: **Checking the results of the plan**

 Researcher A

 Researcher B

 : It would be great to be able to use the entire feather, but unfortunately, [1.](   ) (   )
(   ) (   ).

 : Yes, _____.

 : Do you think we should try a different process?

 : Yes, [2.](   ) (   ) (   )
(   ) (   ) the entire procedure.

A Rearrange the phrases n the parentheses, and fill in the underlined part.

(had / didn't / it / work / as we/ expected)

B Referring to the Japanese below, fill in the blanks 1 and 2.

1. それは上手くいかなかった
2. 私たちは考え直す必要があるかも知れません

C Listen and practice the role play until you can give it fluently.

 Studying further

Trying it out

Practice the conversation by using your own ideas and information.

    A: We should start thinking about replacing _____

    _____ with biodegradable ones.

    B: Yes, but the customers want something that's waterproof.

    A: Well, I've heard about a new material made from surplus chicken feathers.

    B: Really! I'll check into the possibility of using that and also other alternative materials for _____

    _____.

Reviewing

Fill in the blanks by referring to the definitions.

    1. Material used in insulating

                                                         (i _ _ _ _ _ _ _ _)

    2. Birds (such as chickens and ducks) that are raised on farms for their eggs or meat

                                                         (p _ _ _ _ _ _)

    3. Capable of being broken down especially into innocuous products by the action of living things (such as microorganisms)

                                           (b _ _ _ _ _ _ _ _ _ _ _)

UNIT 20

As Web Turns 30, Creator Calls for Big Changes to Make It Better

インターネットの未来は？

 Warming up

☑ インターネットは何を可能にしたか

_____

☑ インターネットの利用における問題は何か

_____

 Understanding technical expressions

Disk2-55, 56

A. Match the English words with the Japanese words.

1. (	) invent	**a.**	伝える
2. (	) transfer	**b.**	利用できること
3. (	) enable	**c.**	発明する
4. (	) browser	**d.**	可能にする
5. (	) availability	**e.**	閲覧ソフト

B. Look at the photo above, and then listen and complete each sentence.

1. Tim Berners-Lee created a way for computers across the world to

(   ) (   ) each other 30 years ago.

（Tim Berners-Lee 氏は、30 年前に世界中のコンピュータが互いにコミュニケーションを取りあう方法を作りだした）

2. He is now calling for big changes to (   ) the World Wide Web (   ) for humanity.

（彼は、現在、World Wide Web を人類にとってより良いものとするよう大きな変化を求めている）

115

The man credited with inventing the World Wide Web 30 years ago is calling for major changes to make it better for humanity.

credited with… 「~の功績が称えられた」

Tim Berners-Lee spoke about the current state of the
5 Web during a 30th anniversary event Tuesday in Geneva, Switzerland. He wrote the first proposal on creating a new system for organizing information. He sent that proposal to a supervisor on March 12, 1989.

supervisor 「上司」

The anniversary event was held at CERN, the
10 European Organization for Nuclear Research. This is the research center where Berners-Lee was working as a computer engineer when he developed his ideas for the World Wide Web.

His proposal sought to create a way for computers
15 across the world to communicate with each other.

The British computer scientist, now 63, had the idea for the hypertext transfer protocol — the "http" in front of each website address. The "http" system enabled the sending and receiving of written information and small
20 images through a software program that became the first web browser. This browser prepared the way for internet availability for large numbers of people through home computers.

Berners-Lee said the Web had clearly created great
25 opportunities for humanity to progress and made life easier for millions of people. It also has given groups traditionally not heard a new voice in society. However, he added that the Web had also provided new ways for "scammers" to carry out crimes and "given a voice to
30 those who spread hatred."

scammer 「詐欺師」

The path to make the internet better is the responsibility of everyone who uses it, Berners-Lee said. Making big changes will not be easy, but will be very well worth it in the end, he added.

worth… 「~の価値がある」

35   "If we give up on building a better Web now, then the Web will not have failed us. We will have failed the Web," he said.

| **fail**… 「〜を失望させる」 |

Taking notes

Read the passage and take notes in Japanese.

  1. Tim Berners-Lee 氏が 30 年前にやったことは何か

_____

_____

_____

  2. Tim Berners-Lee 氏は 1989 年 3 月 12 日に何をしたか

_____

_____

_____

Checking your comprehension

Read the passage and answer the following questions.

  1. Which of the following is stated about an advantage of the World Wide Web?

    a. Sending and receiving written and visual information

    b. Helping people write software programs

    c. Finding ways to investigate crimes

    d. Providing customized computers

  2. Which of the following is stated about a disadvantage of the World Wide Web?

    a. Losing a lot of data

    b. Providing new ways to commit crimes

    c. Manufacturing fake goods

    d. Giving a voice to people who have not been heard

Accepting the challenge

1 | **Practicing pronunciation**  Disk2-58, 59

A 母音に近い音 /w/ の音はよく /u/ の音と区別が難しく、聞き違える場合があります。/w/ は日本語の「ワ」と「ウ」の中間のような音になります。音声を聴き発音してみましょう。

way　　**w**ell　　**w**orth　　**W**orld **W**ide **W**eb

B これまで練習してきたことに注意しながら、以下の文を読んでみましょう。

The "http" system enabled the sending and receiving of written information and small images through a software program that became the first web browser.

2 | **Talking about it** Disk2-60

Plan	Do	Check	**Action**
			まとめ

Stage target focus: **Confirming the performance of a new software program**

 Company executive

 Project leader

1.(　　　　) (　　　　) (　　　　)
(　　　　) (　　　　) (　　　　)
(　　　　) (　　　　) (　　　　) of
designing a new software program?

: Yes, although we have had to make a few revisions due to some unexpected problems.

: I see. But you've managed to 2.(　　　　)
(　　　　) (　　　　) information leaks?

: Yes. Everyone has been very cooperative and we have been able to keep on schedule.

3.(　　　　) (　　　　) (　　　　)
(　　　　). The Board of Directors will be happy to learn about this.

A Listen and complete the conversation.

B Practice the role play until you can give it fluently.

Studying further

Trying it out

Practice the conversation by using your own ideas and information.

A: I hear you've enrolled in graduate school.

B: Yeah. I want to get a master's degree so that _____

_____.

A: Why do you need to do that? You're doing fine right now.

B: Yeah, but _____,

I want to make sure I can keep my job!

A: I'm a little worried about it, too. If I lose my job, I will have to start my own business.

B: Well, that's a good idea.

Reviewing

Fill in the blanks by referring to the definitions.

1. A computer program used for accessing sites or information on a network (such as the World Wide Web)

(b _ _ _ _ _ _)

2. To produce (something, such as a useful device or process) for the first time through the use of the imagination or of ingenious thinking and experiment

(i _ _ _ _ _)

3. To convey from one person, place, or situation to another

(t _ _ _ _ _ _ _)

TEXT PRODUCTION STAFF

| edited by | 編集 |
| Mitsugu Shishido | 宍戸　貢 |

| cover design by | 表紙デザイン |
| Nobuyoshi Fujino | 藤野　伸芳 |

| illustrated by | イラスト |
| Takaichi | タカイチ |

CD PRODUCTION STAFF

narrated by	吹き込み者
Karen Haedrich (Ame E)	カレン・ヘドリック（アメリカ英語）
Dominic Allen(Ame E)	ドミニク・アレン（アメリカ英語）

VOA Science & Technology Report
VOAで学ぶ最先端技術とPBL基礎演習

2020年1月10日　初版発行
2024年2月10日　第6刷発行

著　　者　村尾 純子　深山 晶子
　　　　　野口 ジュディー

発 行 者　佐野 英一郎

発 行 所　株式会社 成 美 堂
　　　　　〒101-0052　東京都千代田区神田小川町3-22
　　　　　TEL 03-3291-2261　FAX 03-3293-5490
　　　　　https://www.seibido.co.jp

印 刷・製 本　倉敷印刷株式会社

ISBN 978-4-7919-7206-7　　　　　　　　　Printed in Japan